Investigating Families and Households

Investigating Families and Households

Nik Jorgensen

Collins Educational
An imprint of HarperCollins*Publishers*

Published by Collins Educational
An imprint of HarperCollins*Publishers*
77–85 Fulham Palace Road
Hammersmith, London W6 8JB

First published in 1995
Reprinted 1996

ISBN 0–00-322407–4

Commissioned by Emma Dunlop
Edited by Louise Wilson and Kay Wright
Production by Jane Bressloff
Cover artwork and design by Derek Lee
Illustrations by Oxford Illustrators
Typeset by Harper Phototypesetters Ltd, Northampton
Printed and bound by Scotprint Ltd, Musselburgh

Contents

Acknowledgements

The author and publisher are indebted to the following::

For permission to reproduce material:

Aspect Picture Library Ltd (Fig 11.4, p168); Basil Blackwell Ltd. (Tab 5.5, p73); British Film Institute (Fig 10.5, p147); Central Statistical Office (Figs 3.3, 4.6, 9.6, 9.8; pp 29, 54, 137, 140; Tabs 9.3, 10.2, 10.3, pp125, 148,); Economist Publications (Fig 11.6, p173); Format Partners Picture Library (Figs 9.2, 11.3; pp113, 163); Guardian Media Group PLC (Fig 8.1, 10.1, 10.6; pp100, 142, 149); Isle of Wight Tourism (photo p13); Macmillan Publishers (Tab 5.4, p71); Mary Evans Picture Library (Fig 10.2, p142); Nigel Paige (Figs 1.4, 4.7, 8.2, 10.4, 11.2; pp8, 50, 101, 145, 162); O.P.C.S. (Fig 4.8, 8.3, 9.6, Item E, Fig 10.3, 10.7, 11.1, 11.2; pp54, 103, 137, 140, 144, 151, 160, 161; Tabs 10.2, 10.3, p148), Photofusion (Figs 4.6, 8.4; pp47, 106); Polity Press (Fig 5.4, p68); Private Eye (Fig 4.5, p47); Reed Book Service (Wine Bar, pp59-60); Rex Features (Fig 1.2, p4); Solo Syndication (Figs 1.1, 5.1; pp2), 60); The Bridgeman Art LIbrary (Figs 2.3, 4.2; pp16, 46); Topham Picture Library (Figs 2.4, 2.5, 2.7; pp17, 19, 21); University of London Examination And Assessment Council (Stimulus-response questions, p13); Van den Bergh Foods (Fig 7.1, p94), Welsh Industrial Museum (Fig 2.6, p20).

We are especially grateful to Mark Kirby, Francine Koubel and Nick Madry for the Stimulus-response questions appearing at the end of Chapters 2, 3, 6, 9 and 11. These questions first appeared in *Sociology: Developing Skills Through Structured Questions*, Collins Educational, 1993

Introduction

'One of the key problems of our time is how we bring up the next generation of children.'

(Professor A.H. Halsey, 1994)

The aim of this book is to provide an in-depth study of families and households from a sociological viewpoint. The subject matter of sociology is society, and it is often said that the family is the most important social unit. The United Nations designated 1994 as the Year of the Family. In Western societies such as Britain, the USA and some European countries a variety of commentators ranging from politicians to media personnel to religious leaders regularly make pronouncements about the modern family. In such societies there appear to be mixed feelings about what is happening to families and households.

A range of views on the family

Praise for the family comes from these sources, among others:

- Religious leaders often comment positively on the role of the family. The leader of the Roman Catholic Church, the Pope, suggested early in 1994 that the family was the key to world peace.

- Fairy stories, romantic novels and similar fiction often idealize the family in the context of romantic love. Typically the story ends when the hero and heroine are married, and then 'they lived happily ever after'.

- Advertising often presents the stereotypical nuclear family of breadwinner husband and dependent wife and children in a cosy, romanticized manner.

Other views concerning the family have come from a variety of sources:

- Politicians have highlighted the breakdown of the family as a cause of a number of social ills, particularly the rising crime rate.

- Some commentators and sections of the press linked the extreme and unusual case of the two 10-year-old murderers of the toddler, James Bulger, in Liverpool in 1993 to dysfunctional aspects of their families.

- Increasingly frequent reports of the extent of domestic violence against wives and children, and of young children being left at home to fend for themselves (the

'Home Alone' phenomenon of the early 1990s), have added to a gloomier portrait of life in modern families.

- The costs to the state and the taxpayer of single parenthood have been highlighted by Conservative politicians in Britain.

- Marital breakdowns among the Royal Family (as they are perhaps unfortunately known), most notably Prince Charles and Princess Diana, have made world headlines.

Figure 1.1 Charles and Diana in Korea during their last tour together

In the light of these contradictory messages, what is the true condition of the family today? Surveys tell us that despite frequent negative publicity about the family, a happy and contented family life is what most people desire. A high proportion of divorcees remarry despite their previous experience. Children of unhappy or broken marriages go on to marry and form their own families.

Clearly we are dealing with a highly complex social institution. Both individuals and society as a whole seem to be confused in their attitudes to the family, uncertain how to assess its success or failure and how to respond to the changes it seems to be undergoing.

Four out of ten contemporary marriages will end in divorce, but five out of ten will reach their silver wedding anniversary (25 years). In two or three sentences, explain this apparent paradox, using some of the points made in the previous section.

Sociological approaches to families and households

This book focuses on families and households rather than 'the family' to convey the diversity and variety of ways in which people live their personal lives. When we talk about 'the family' as a sociological concept it quickly becomes apparent that it is problematic. The following activities explore some of the difficulties.

1 Working if possible in pairs or small groups, complete the following statement: 'The family is . . . '

2 When you have completed this sentence, identify the core components of your definition and make a list of them.

3 Now, on your own, complete the following statement: 'My family is . . . '

4 List the key features of your own family and compare them with your first list.

5 Return to your partner or small group and exchange ideas about the differences, if any, that you have found between your two lists.

6 Summarize the key points that emerge from this discussion and present them to the whole class.

Your work on the previous activity will probably have illustrated some of the complexities that definitions of 'the family' involve. It would now be useful to conduct a small survey among relatives, friends and other students to obtain a wider view. This will give you the chance to develop further your perspective on the issues, and it will also set you thinking about how to conduct sociological research.

Design an appropriate questionnaire (you may need to consult library sources on sociological research for this), which can be in the form of questions or a list of statements for respondents to rank in order as appropriate. The following are examples of statements you might want to use; you should be able to devise up to ten altogether:

The family is:

1 A married couple living with their children.

2 A divorced woman living with her children.

3 A group of students renting a house together.

This activity could be widened and further developed to make a more detailed sociological project.

If we try to examine our own mental image of 'the family', we can probably conjure up pictures of marriage, raising children, relationships between husbands and wives, monogamy and fidelity, key figures such as grandparents, aunts, uncles, cousins and so on. Depending on your own experiences of family life, such images may be positive, negative or even ambivalent. Some sociologists focus on key aspects of this mental imagery to stress the more positive institutional aspects of the family and its contribution to social order and equilibrium. Other sociologists stress the more negative aspects of the family, perhaps focusing on inequalities between husbands and wives and parents and children.

Figure 1.2 A typical family?

Sociology and objectivity

Sociology as a social science discipline aims to be objective in approach to its subject matter. Clearly an institution such as the family, which is probably one of the closest to us emotionally, raises problems when we study it in an academic manner. As a student of the family you need to examine your own experiences and feelings about the family to gain a deeper understanding of your subject.

It has often been said that the best sociology treats the everyday as 'anthropologically strange' – in other words, you should treat your own society as if it were an unknown tribe. A similar idea is that of the 'Martian perspective' where you view the social world as if you were an alien being. The difference in both cases of course is that you are yourself a member of the society you are studying, so such perspectives can only act as a framework or guideline.

One of the key figures in the development of sociology, Max Weber, recognized such issues of objectivity. He advocated *'verstehen'* (the ability to see the world through other people's eyes) combined with scientific and objective rigour. So 'investigating families and households' means investigating your own personal experiences and applying to them the knowledge provided in this book in as dispassionate a manner as possible.

> *Make a list of the sorts of things that make an objective study of the family difficult.*

Theoretical approaches to the family

Reflecting the differences of opinion found in the world at large, sociological approaches range from those that are positive about the role of the family in society to those that are strongly negative and see the family as a damaging social institution. Figure 1.3 represents the range of views involved.

Positive		Negative
Functionalism	Liberal feminism	Radical psychiatry
	Marxist feminism	Radical feminism
	Feminist Marxism	Ultra-radical feminism

Figure 1.3 The range of views on the family

Functionalist theories of the family

We shall be examining these theories in depth in Chapter 3. In brief, they hold that the family 'fits' the needs of an advanced industrial society. They see society as comparable to a biological organism, in which social institutions such as the family contribute to the stability or equilibrium of the whole.

Functionalist theorists, then, take a very positive view of the family, for they hold that it meets well the needs of an advanced industrial society for a geographically and socially mobile workforce. One family structure in particular, the nuclear family comprising a breadwinner husband and dependent wife and children, is singled out as the ideal type for a modern society. US sociologists in particular have developed this approach, notably Murdock, Parsons and Goode.

The functionalist school has been accused by its critics of being ideological in tone and representing a conservative stance. Some feminists highlight the 'familial ideology' epitomized by such approaches – in other words, it presents an image and ideal of family life that does not represent real experience, particularly that of women, whom feminists see as oppressed by the family.

However, its defenders claim that the functionalist view of family life is shared by many people, at least as an aspiration.

 From your own experience, how typical of modern family life is the nuclear family as portrayed by functionalist sociologists?

Marxist approaches

We shall be examining Marxist theories in detail in Chapter 4. According to this approach, the family is an instrument of oppression and exploitation, particularly of women, that serves the interests of a capitalist society.

Marxist approaches have been divided into Marxist-Feminist and Feminist-Marxist. The former is linked with more traditional Marxism, and sees the role of the family under capitalism as primarily economically exploitative: the family supports and comforts the (male) 'wage slave' through the exploited and unpaid labour of his wife, who acts in a serving and servicing role. Meals are provided, children are looked after and the housework is done without payment. This helps to reduce wage demands upon the capitalist, thus indirectly increasing profits.

The Feminist-Marxist approach sees the family as an ideological institution that has associated with it a set of beliefs, ideas and expectations. Typical of such beliefs are the idea that social inequality is inevitable, and that the proper role of women is to be good housewives and mothers. Such values are passed on through the family from generation to generation.

Marxists envisage the eventual ending of capitalism, resulting in a communist or socialist society where men and women are equal and exploitation and oppression in the family and elsewhere are ended. In practice, earlier Marxist societies such as post-revolutionary Russia after 1917 insisted on women working alongside men on an equal basis.

Critics of such approaches say that in reality exploitation and oppression, particularly of women, still continue and are a feature of all societies, whether capitalist or Marxist, industrial or tribal. The overthrow of capitalism does not necessarily alleviate the problems of family life as identified.

 Working in pairs, make a list of points to contribute to a class discussion on the applicability of the Marxist approach to the modern family as you experience it. You could examine whether exploitation of wives is a key feature of the family and the ideas associated with it. Alternatively, make your own notes on such issues.

Non-Marxist feminist approaches

As we shall see in more detail in Chapter 5, feminist theorists have exposed some of the weaknesses of the Marxist approaches briefly referred to above. Instead of seeing the key to the explanation of women's oppression as being the exploitative nature of family life under *capitalism*, this view focuses on the concept of *patriarchy*.

In a patriarchal society, power and authority are held by males. For instance, in the workplace most managers and authority figures are male. This power structure is reflected in the organization of the family, where males (husbands, brothers, sons) dominate and are served and serviced by females (wives, sisters, daughters), who are exploited and oppressed by this structure.

Non-Marxist feminists do not see the overthrow of capitalism as the answer to inequality in family relationships, but see the answer as being a change in the relationship between men and women. Two views emerge from this – liberal feminism and radical feminism.

Liberal feminists can be described as gradualist. They believe that change is gradually occurring, and through persuasion women are slowly getting men to become more involved in sharing household and childrearing tasks. This view is echoed in the concept of the symmetrical family (see pages 67-8), in which the traditional family has evolved or is evolving towards a more egalitarian institution with husbands and wives participating equally in family life.

 Do you think that most families are symmetrical today? Are they moving in that direction?

Some radical feminists see no possibility of such a change occurring within present society because it is the family itself, and its associated patriarchal structures benefiting men, that are the root cause of women's oppression. True liberation for women can only result from the abolition of the family and patriarchy.

Some advocates of this viewpoint envisage a society without families, and some even wish to create a society without men. The latter may at present seem to belong in the realms of science fiction where all-female societies with sperm banks, selective gender reproduction and artificial insemination are possible. However, it should be noted that although the 'maleless societies' view may appear extreme, such 'reproductive technologies' are already available to some women.

Critics of such views see them as anti-male and rooted in lesbian politics with utopian dreams of an all-female future.

> *Organize a class debate or make notes examining the two views presented above, addressing the question: 'True liberation for women can only come about by the abolition of the family.'*

Radical psychiatry

As we shall explore in Chapter 6, radical psychiatrists have generally offered a gloomy view of family life, and have focused on the family as the main source of human unhappiness. According to this view, the family stifles individuality because of the control parents exercise over their children, hampering their development in the direction of becoming free-thinking, autonomous individuals.

Pioneers of this approach, such as R.D. Laing and David Cooper (both psychiatrists by background), have linked mental illnesses such as schizophrenia to the repressive nature of family life. They saw the family as a hotbed of emotional blackmail, psychologically suffocating for its members, particularly growing children.

Characteristic of this approach is an emphasis on the dark side of the family, highlighting violence and physical and sexual abuse as features of life in families.

Critics of such views see them as somewhat overdrawn. They admit the negative aspects that radical psychiatry has tended to highlight, but maintain that these are minority experiences; families in which such behaviour is common are 'dysfunctional' or not working properly, so the answer is to seek the root cause within the families concerned rather than ascribing such problems to families as a whole. R.D. Laing himself acknowledged a few years before his death in 1989 that he had gained a lot from his own family experiences.

Phenomenological or interpretive approaches

Apart from radical psychiatry, the approaches we have discussed so far can be described as macro or structuralist in emphasis: they analyse the family in terms of its role within society on a grand scale and do not concern themselves with the everyday world of individual families. According to the interpretive perspective, as we shall explore in Chapter 7, the key to understanding the family lies in the interaction, negotiation and role expectations, with their associated meanings, of members as they live out their daily lives together.

Rather than seeing society as the key unit of analysis, interpretivists concentrate on the daily interaction in families and examine how gender roles, husband–wife relationships, child behaviour and so on are socially constructed. This analysis can be couched in terms of meanings associated with family roles; for instance, what does a wife mean when she says she has a 'good husband'? Negotiated ideas and common-sense understandings of what it means to be a family and to live as a family are examined.

The research carried out from this perspective is small-scale and observational, aiming to gather qualitative data from time-budget diaries, in-depth interviews and close involvement. The sociologist Liz Stanley visited and closely observed a family in

Figure 1.4 A 'fly on the wall' sociologist

Rochdale every day for several weeks in order to gain the insights that this type of study requires.

Recent television documentaries on families and households made in Australia (*Sylvania Waters*) and Britain (*FamilyWatch*) have used 'fly on the wall' techniques, with television camera crews living with families for several months at a time, to give viewers a similarly intimate picture.

Obviously in such a personal and private arena as the family this type of research is extremely difficult to carry out and it is not surprising that there have been few studies in this field so far.

Critics of this approach who follow a traditionally scientific or positivistic line point to the subjectivity and small scale of such research, which makes generalization and a fuller understanding of the role of the family in society very difficult.

New Right approaches

According to the New Right, as we shall see in Chapter 8, a strong family unit with a loving married couple and their dependent children is the key to a healthy society.

The term New Right covers contributions from a number of fields and various origins outside sociology in conservative moral philosophy, monetarist economics, fundamentalist religious movements and conservative political groups. In Britain such influences are associated with Thatcherism, in the USA with the politics of the former President Ronald Reagan, and there are similar political movements in other parts of the world.

This group holds a pessimistic view of the current state of society and desires to return to a former 'Golden Age' – Mrs Thatcher sometimes seemed to identify this with Victorian Britain – when things were supposedly much better than they are today. Conservatives in Britain have blamed the present deterioration they perceive on earlier 'left-wing' or 'socialist' governments, declining moral standards, young people, the failure of the education system, the values of the 1960s generation and related 'social problems'. Their ideal family – a strong unit composed of loving parents and their children – is believed to be the key to the health and well-being of society in the future.

Sociologically these views can be linked to functionalism, which has its roots in the work of Emile Durkheim. His concept of *anomie* (normlessness, the breakdown of common-core values in society) is relevant to the thinking associated with New Right approaches.

Not all sociological contributions on the decline of the family have been associated with the political Right. Similar concerns have been expressed by eminent figures such as Professor A.H. Halsey and Dr Norman Dennis, who describe themselves as ethical socialists. Halsey and Dennis have focused on the rise of 'fatherless families' in current times, and have maintained that children of such families attain less educationally than the average, are more likely to be involved in crime, suffer poorer health and have other associated social problems.

Criticisms of such views, whether of the political Right or not, are similar to those levelled at functionalist approaches in that the desired and idealized model of family life portrayed is not the reality for most people. A 'Golden Age' is a historically dubious concept as there is little doubt that family life has always been as variable and as potentially fraught with conflict as it is today. The family of Dickens's time cannot seriously be held up as the model of correctness that New Right thinkers aspire to in modern family life.

 Carry out research using newspapers, and CD-ROM if available, into any reporting of family issues that could possibly be associated with New Right ideas.

Couples should stay together for children

Elizabeth Hess, 30, is a full-time mother of two: to four-year-old William and Emily, 18 months. Her husband Edward is a barrister and they live in Kensington. She says:

Moral values should be taught by parents. But if nobody has taught *them* they can't teach their children.

Nowadays, we need good, strong nursery schools to fill the gaps. I also believe sex education should teach children not only how to produce babies but also what to do with them once they are born. It's preferable, if not always necessary, for parents to be married.

But it is very important that parents stay together while their children grow up, even if they argue.

Divorce is more harmful to children than living in a home where they feel stable but where there are lots of arguments. Mothers should work if they want to, but it's a lot harder being a full-time mother than having a child and going out to work.

Daily Express, 9 March 1994

The family, families or households?

The reason for using the phrase 'families and households' in the title of this book, rather than simply 'the family', has already been briefly explained. This section considers the issues in more detail.

What do we mean when we use the word 'family'?

- Are we referring to people who live together in a household and have a relationship to each other through ties of blood, marriage or adoption?

- What about our 'wider' family and relations, such as grandparents, aunts, uncles and cousins who do not live in the same household as us?

- A household may be a group of people (such as students) who share accommodation and facilities for eating and washing, but are they a 'family'?

1 *In Bengali there are fifty-three different terms for a relative; in English we work with a dozen basic terms. Explain the difference.*

2 *What are the twelve or so English terms?*

3 *Define 'second cousin twice removed'.*

Like natural scientists, sociologists try to categorize the subject under study, so precise descriptive and definitional terms such as 'nuclear family', 'step-family', 'extended family' and 'one-parent family' are used. The glossary at the end of this chapter provides you with the definitions of such terms.

The fact that so many such terms are necessary would suggest that rather than 'the family' we should speak of 'families' and 'households', because we need to capture the diversity of ways in which the majority of people live and have relationships described as 'family' with each other.

Stronger criticisms of a concentration on the family, with its implication that this is the 'natural' domestic unit, come from a number of sources. Feminists and those of a leftist political stance would prefer that households became the focus of studies of how people live their personal and private lives. Such critics point to the variability of how people live today. For instance:

- approximately 25 per cent of British households are occupied by one person;

- approximately 20 per cent of British households are occupied by a married couple with dependent children.

Constant emphasis on 'the family' has normative and ideological overtones which cast non-family dwellers as 'outsiders' and 'deviants'.

However, replacing the term 'family' with 'household' is also unsatisfactory as it implies a focus on the person or people living in a single residence. Clearly this denies key features of the family, which extends beyond the bounds of a common residence. When we consider the family we are looking at relationships that cut across households, with obligations that are not determined by shared living arrangements.

The British sociologist Robert Chester has argued strongly that despite household composition studies exposing the proportionately few stereotypical nuclear families (breadwinner husband, dependent wife and children), when their overall lifetime experience (sometimes referred to as the life cycle or life course) is considered most people have or will have experience of family life for the majority of the time. Chapter 11 provides more detail on this argument.

 Consider the life course (biography) of an older relative who now lives alone. Does Chester's argument apply to them?

It is hoped that reading this book will convey to you that the idea of 'the family' is not something fixed, or even easily defined and explained. Throughout the world, not just in Britain and similar societies, the family and its associated relationships are complex and sometimes confusing social phenomena exhibiting a wide variety of forms, structures and types that reflect the diversity of arrangements by which we may raise children and live in close personal relationships with each other.

The usefulness of sociology

Sociology is the social scientific study of society, and as such it approaches its subject matter as objectively as possible, providing evidence for its conclusions from empirical research. The aim is to provide a picture of social change and the way people live together in the modern world. The theoretical approaches introduced in this chapter attempt to explain systematically the role of the family within society and its relationship to other key social institutions.

Empirical studies of families and households can give insights that help to build up a wider picture of the working of the family. By presenting the more negative phenomena currently surrounding the family, such as rising divorce rates, as widespread social phenomena, sociology also helps us to see them as what the American sociologist C. Wright Mills called 'public issues', rather than simply as 'personal troubles' for which individuals are to blame.

 Discuss in pairs or make notes on C. Wright Mills's distinction between 'public issues' and 'personal troubles'. Use the current divorce rate – four in ten of today's marriages ending in divorce – to consider how divorce can be seen as more of a social than a personal problem.

Feminist sociologists have contributed to a raised awareness of the inegalitarian and male-orientated aspects of family life as it is experienced by many people. For the husband or father the family may offer a rewarding and joyful experience, but for many wives and mothers the family can be a source of stress brought about by the demands of childcare and household tasks which are not greatly shared by most men.

We have touched upon a number of aspects of families and households in this introductory chapter. In the rest of the book we shall explore a variety of ways of looking at the family from a sociological viewpoint to give you as full a portrait as possible of a complex and fascinating social institution that has profound effects on our lives.

Glossary

This introductory chapter has illustrated the limitations of words like 'family', 'families' and 'households' when used in a sociological context. A sociologist studying such a complex social institution needs a more precise terminology, in much the same way as a zoologist does when studying the complexities of the animal world. The glossary below defines some of the more common terms used in this area of sociology.

Bigamy The act of going through a marriage ceremony with someone while being lawfully married to someone else; this is a crime in Britain and can result in up to seven years' imprisonment.

Bourgeois family Literally means a middle-class family, but in recent times is used in a somewhat disparaging way to refer to an inward-looking, isolated, consumption-orientated nuclear family that is predominantly concerned with its own members and not the wider world outside. Such a family is neatly summed up in Margaret Thatcher's infamous statement, 'There is no such thing as society; there are only individual men and women, and there are families.'

Clan family Similar to the extended family, but can involve a group of nuclear families related to each other living somewhat independently in separate accommodation but in close proximity.

Cohabitation An unmarried couple who live together and have a sexual relationship. In the past this was often seen as a temporary phase, a 'trial' period before marriage which usually happened when pregnancy occurred. More recently there is evidence of long-term cohabitation in Western societies, where increasing numbers of unmarried couples are raising children.

Divorce The legal termination of a marriage.

Extended family More than two generations living in a household. The term **modified extended family** describes the more recent situation where extended family members live in close proximity to each other, i.e. in the same neighbourhood.

Family A group of people tied by relationships of blood, marriage or adoption.

Family of origin The family you are born into and grow up in.

Family of procreation The family formed in adulthood, e.g. after a person leaves the family of origin's residence, marries and has children, usually forming a nuclear family.

Household A residence for one person or a group of people, who can be a family or unrelated, sharing aspects of the accommodation such as communal eating facilities.

Monogamy Marriage to or cohabitation with one partner.

Nuclear family Husband, wife and children living in the same residence. Can be described as traditional or stereotypical, with the husband as breadwinner with a dependent wife and children. The **modified nuclear family** refers to the more common recent situation where mothers and fathers both work and have children.

One-parent (single-parent/lone-parent) family/household Can be an unmarried mother, often associated with unwanted pregnancy in the younger age group, more frequently a divorced woman with her dependent children. About 10 per cent are headed by a lone male.

Polygamy Marriage to more than one partner; this is legal in many societies, e.g. a number of Muslim countries, but in practice is in decline. There are two forms of polygamy: **polygyny,** denoting a man with more than one wife, the more common form of polygamy; or **polyandry,** in which a woman takes more than one husband (usually brothers) at a time; this arrangement is very rare, but can occur in remote nomadic tribal societies, e.g. in mountainous regions of Nepal, where men are away on long absences tending herds.

Separation When a marriage breaks down and the former partners live apart. Today this is usually a preliminary period before divorce, but in the past, when divorce was difficult to obtain, separation was for many people a lifelong condition.

Serial monogamy As divorce rates have risen, increasing numbers of people are remarrying, and during their life cycle may have a succession of monogamous relationships.

Step-family (reconstituted/reordered family) Family formed as a result of remarriage of one or both partners to which they bring children from former relationships.

Symmetrical family Identified by Young and Wilmott as a type of family evolving in the late twentieth century in which husbands and wives have a more egalitarian relationship in the home; household and childrearing activities are increasingly shared.

List of general textbooks

You will need to consult the following general textbooks for further reading at appropriate points as you work through this book:

Abbott, P. and Wallace, C. (1990) *An Introduction to Sociology*, London: Routledge

Bilton, T. *et al.* (1987) *Introductory Sociology*, 2nd edn, Basingstoke: Macmillan

Giddens, A. (1978) *Durkheim*, Glasgow: Fontana

—— (1993) *Sociology*, 2nd edn, Cambridge: Polity Press

Haralambos, M. and Holborn, M. (1995) *Sociology: Themes and Perspectives*, 4th edn, London: Collins Educational

McNeill, P. and Townley, C. (1986) *Fundamentals of Sociology*, 2nd edn, London: Macmillan

O'Donnell, M. (1992) *A New Introduction to Sociology*, 3rd edn, Walton-on-Thames: Nelson

Parkin, F. (1982) *Max Weber*, London: Tavistock

Wright Mills, C. (1959) *The Sociological Imagination*, New York: Oxford University Press

Stimulus – response questions

Consider the stimulus material above and answer the questions that follow:

(a) What is the difference between a 'family' and a 'household'? **(4 marks)**

(b) Why is it always important to make this distinction between 'family' and 'household' when carrying out research into the extended family? **(4 marks)**

(c) A growing proportion of the population lives alone. What changes in family, household or other social patterns explain this? **(7 marks)**

(d) Assess the view that images used by the advertising industry, such as the one above, support and sustain a particular model of family life. **(10 marks)**

Total: 25 marks

Historical approaches to families and households

Key ideas

- Evolutionary approach
- Childhood in the twentieth century
- Industrialization and urbanization
- Nuclear households in the past
- Industrial working-class extended families
- The 'lonely city'
- Privatization of the family and household
- Loss of community

Key figures

- Tamara K. Hareven
- P.I. Sorokin
- Philippe Aries
- Peter Laslett
- Michael Anderson
- M. Young and P. Wilmott
- Edward Shorter
- Richard Sennett
- Ferdinand Mount

Until relatively recently it was widely accepted by sociologists that the present form and structure of the modern family had evolved from an earlier extended type that was predominant in pre-industrial societies. The modern nuclear family emerged as a result of the processes of industrialization and urbanization.

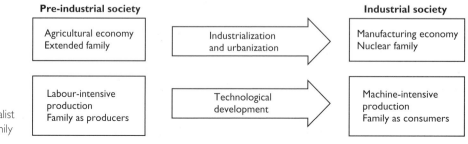

Figure 2.1 The functionalist view of the evolving family

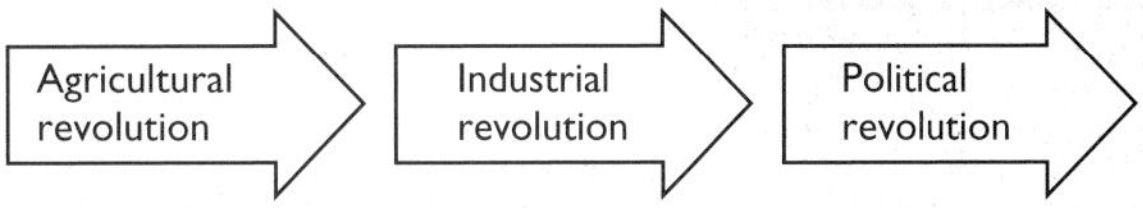

Figure 2.2 The Marxist view of the evolving family

	Primitive communism	Feudalism	Capitalism	Socialism
Production	Hunter-gatherer bands	Landowners and serfs	Owners and workers	Common ownership
Stratification	Classless society	Aristocracy and peasantry	Bourgeoisie and proletariat	Classless society
Authority	Matriarchy	Patriarchy		Equality
Context of reproduction	Group marriage	Extended family	Nuclear family	Community family

This evolutionary view was particularly emphasized by functionalist sociologists (see Chapter 3). Marxist sociologists (see Chapter 4) have also emphasized the evolution of the present nuclear family from earlier forms, but see the 'cause' of this to be capitalism rather than industrialization.

Family historian Tamara K. Hareven (1994, p. 14) summarizes the dominant view:

> Sociologists in particular argued that, in pre-industrial societies, the dominant household form had contained an extended family, often involving three co-resident generations, and that the 'modern' family, characterized by a nuclear household structure, family limitation, the spacing of children, and population mobility, was the product of industrialization.

It is to some extent true to say that living in a form of nuclear family is a dominant experience for many in a modern society. However, the assumption of a dominant experience of an extended family in the past has been questioned in recent years as a result of the work of a number of family historians. Work in such fields as historical demography (population trends) and qualitative documentary research unearthing details of how people resided together in the past has brought into question many traditional assumptions. Significant contributions to this debate have been made by Philippe Aries, Peter Laslett and Michael Anderson, whose work will be considered later in this chapter along with that of other relevant writers.

One of the earliest influences on the evolutionary view that functionalist sociologists such as Parsons adopted was P.I. Sorokin (1889–1968) who suggested that urban growth associated with industrialization had resulted in the formation of the small nuclear family which was a result of the fragmentation of the earlier extended family (Sorokin 1959). Parsons (1954) saw this in a positive sense as an adaptation to social changes that required a smaller, more 'mobile' family unit. His views will be explored in more detail in the next chapter.

Support for the traditional sociological view

Philippe Aries, a French historian, carried out detailed studies of the changing nature of childhood and the family in France and England from pre-modern to modern

Figure 2.3 Child as 'miniature adult'

times (Aries 1960). He suggested that childhood as we know it – by which he meant the idea of a 'child' identity separate from that of adults – was essentially a creation of the present century. His argument was that in previous times children were effectively miniature adults and were treated as such.

The art historian, John Berger, has supported this view by demonstrating that in paintings of earlier centuries children are portrayed as 'miniature adults' by their posture, dress and demeanour (see Berger 1972).

Do your own research on this by visiting a local art gallery and looking for early family portraits to see if the 'miniature adult' view is correct. Can you find any modern paintings that portray children in a different way?

Historical sociologists such as Richard Sennett (1977) have pointed out how in the past 'games' and 'play' were not separate 'childhood' activities but things in which adults participated, and they too took an interest in dolls' houses and dresses and model soldiers.

Can you think of any modern examples of games or toys that adults share with children?

A contemporary illustration of the way that children's and adults' games are treated as separate from one another can be seen in computer games. Games that are aimed at adults are often described as 'relaxing' or 'stimulating', whereas many children's games are considered trivial and inane. Adults express concern that children use computers to play 'games' rather than engaging in more serious educational activities. This separateness of the child's world from that of adults would have been inconceivable to people in earlier centuries, according to Aries and others.

In the past, people lived in larger dwellings – the 'big house' where 'people lived on top of one another, masters and servants, children and adults, in houses open at all hours to the indiscretions of the callers' (Aries 1960). This picture is reinforced by Emmanuel Le Roy Ladurie, a French historian whose classic study of life in a medieval French village highlighted the importance of the 'Domus' or household that was occupied by a range of adults and children, related and unrelated, all contributing to the maintenance and support of each other (Ladurie 1990).

The main focus of the household was sociability rather than privacy. The notion of privacy and intimacy between a small group of people within the confines of the parent–child nuclear family is a twentieth-century concept. Children in the past were in a household relationship with a wider range of adults, and the roles they played and the tasks they carried out were similar to those that the adults performed, such as tending animals, planting crops and harvesting.

This pattern continued into the earlier stages of industrialization, until the nineteenth-century Child Labour Acts increasingly restricted children's work in mills and factories. In Britain in 1870 the Forster Education Act introduced compulsory schooling provided by the State, so the historical trend has been towards a separation of the child from the world of the adult.

Figure 2.4 Children selling onions, Plymouth, c. 1907

Consult books of historical photographs to find portraits of children working. List the range of occupations portrayed.

A feature of these changes is a new conception of children as being in need of care and protection for a longer period than merely early infancy. Marxists and feminists (see Chapter 4) have highlighted how this significantly changed the role of women into that of exploited childcarer and homemaker within what we now identify as the nuclear family unit. The trend of increasing protection of children within the parental home has continued in the twentieth century. Sennett (1993) traces its origins to the eighteenth century, when the idea of a stable personality for children was linked to their closer relationship to fewer adults, notably their mother and father rather than the wider group of kin and associated adults.

Arguments against the evolutionary perspective

Peter Laslett was one of the first and most significant figures to question 'conventional wisdom' concerning the changed nature of families and households through time. He was a founder of the Cambridge Family History Group which carried out detailed demographic studies of European countries in earlier centuries using historical documents such as parish records and population census data.

Laslett (1972) found that, contrary to traditional sociological views, the extended family household was not a dominant type in the past, particularly in Western Europe where the nuclear family household was more typical. Evidence for this was based on average per head household size, which Laslett found was not dramatically different from today's. One-parent families (see Chapter 10), which are often seen as a modern phenomenon, were also common in the past.

 Use your textbooks and library sources to collect as much information as you can about Laslett's work, and make summary notes of your findings.

What was the reason for the existence of most one-parent families in the past, and how does this differ from one-parent families today?

Visit an old graveyard and see what evidence you can gather, from inscriptions on gravestones, about the nature of family life in the past, such as the premature death of spouses and children.

Michael Anderson provides another challenge to the evolutionary view, but from a different perspective. He studied households in Preston, a textile area, using data from the 1851 Census, and found that contrary to expectations extended families were fairly common (Anderson 1981). Older relatives in households could care for younger children while their parents went out to work in the mills, and in return they eventually received care in their old age. Anderson also identified the practice of taking in orphans, who were cared for and in turn could contribute to the household with their working wages. Other historians have also pointed to the practice of households taking in lodgers, usually young males who worked away from home.

A portrait emerges from such work of a household that is rather similar to earlier households — the 'big house' referred to by Aries and the 'Domus' highlighted by Le Roy Ladurie. This particularly calls into question the idea that the process of industrialization broke up the extended family and replaced it with the nuclear family.

Why might industrialization lead to the break-up of the extended family? Discuss in pairs or write your own response, focusing on rural compared to urban life and geographical movements of populations in the early stages of industrialization.

Figure 2.5 Extended East
End family in the 1950s

In *The Family and Kinship in East London* (1965), a study of an East End community carried out in the 1950s, Michael Young and Peter Wilmott highlighted the continued existence and importance of the extended family in working-class neighbourhoods. The pattern of mutual help and support within and between households as a way of coping with low wages and hardship seemed to be very like that emerging from Anderson's study of nineteenth-century Preston.

Other community studies carried out in the 1960s, such as *Coal Is Our Life* (Dennis, Henriques and Slaughter 1956) and *The Fisherman* (Tunstall 1962), found comparable patterns of extended family living. A common reason for such a pattern was the mutual benefit and support provided, particularly in circumstances of insecurity, low wages and poverty. So for many people, particularly the urbanized industrial working class, industrialization did not result in a nuclear family household.

Some family historians, such as Tamara K. Hareven, have used these themes to put forward an argument in opposition to Parsons and other functionalist writers. They point out that the nuclear family is somewhat dysfunctional for an industrial society, because discipline in the workplace and opportunities for jobs could be better controlled by extended families than by the nuclear family. The (traditionally male) breadwinner in an isolated nuclear family could be drawn into agitating for higher wage levels to support 'his' family, i.e. dependent wife and children, and industrial action such as strikes might result. A network of older family members, in contrast, could calm down such 'hot-headed' impulses, the result being to the benefit of the employer (Hareven 1994). So extended families could be seen as functional for an industrial society because of their contribution to workplace stability.

Another point that applies to this debate is the way the extended family can contribute to labour continuity through recruitment from family members. Until

Figure 2.6 Two generations of miners

relatively recently it was common knowledge that your ability to get a job in many occupations and industries such as mining, shipbuilding and the docks could be enhanced if you had relatives who worked there: having a word with the foreman or supervisor when younger family members reached working age was a common practice. This remains true in some areas, and not only among traditional working-class occupations: similar patterns can be found in more middle-class working environments such as banks, offices and medical schools, where a family link can be a useful connection. As the saying goes, 'It's not what you know, it's who you know.'

Consider the examples just given of how extended families can help younger members to obtain work. How widely does this argument still apply today? Discuss in small groups or pairs, or write down your reply. Use examples from your own families or acquaintances.

The idea of the development of privacy and sentiment in family life that originated in the work of Aries was further developed by Edward Shorter (1975). In some senses the work of both Shorter and Aries appears to lend support to earlier and simpler 'before' and 'after' evolutionary approaches to the family, but they differ in several ways. Shorter attempts in a comprehensive manner to demonstrate a trend in family life throughout Europe towards the greater separateness and distinctiveness of the conjugally based family. Features of this process include:

- the growth of romantic love;

- the development of motherhood as a full-time and largely separate occupation;

- a focus on the married couple as the basis of family life;

- idealization of the married couple with dependent children;

- promotion of the home-centred household as the sole source of private, personal relationships.

Shorter defines 'sentiment' in the following terms:

- partner selection based on romantic love;

Figure 2.7 Crowds on
Waterloo Bridge

- mother–infant relationships and an emphasis on maternal love;

- privacy and intimacy within the household.

The historian Lawrence Stone notes, however, that some of these developments that were the basis of modern family life were established before the onset of industrialization (Stone 1990). This supports Laslett's views and goes against the functionalist approach, which sees the privatized nuclear family of modern times as a product of the process of industrialization.

Historians such as Stone and Shorter are not presenting a picture of a change from an extended family form to a nuclear family form, but rather perceive an overall shift in patterns of control and in the relationships within the family and between the family and the wider society. The main features they identify are:

- a shift in emphasis from issues of descent and lineage to a stress on marriage and conjugality;

- a shift from vertical relationships (parental authority over children) to horizontal relationships (egalitarian/democratic decision making).

They link such developments to changes in meaning associated with the family. They also point to:

- a weakening of community controls over domestic relationships;

- a greater distinction between the public and the private.

Explain each of these in more detail, giving examples.

A number of historians and sociologists have pointed to the growth of the distinction between public and private spheres in the twentieth century. It has been associated with the growth of urban areas, as highlighted by the Chicago School of sociologists earlier in the century. One of them, Louis Wirth, depicted the loneliness and isolation of city life for many people (Wirth 1938). Some scholars focused on the decline or death of community with the growth of urbanization and people's increasing retreat into a private world in which only a few close personal relationships developed.

> *Do you agree that loneliness and isolation are features of city life? If so, how might this make family life more private and important?*

Sennett (1993) traces such developments back to earlier centuries when public life in towns and cities was comparable to a theatre stage. People paraded, posed and engaged in conversation with strangers very much like actors on a stage. This was reflected in elaborate dress and the wearing of wigs and face powder among males. During the nineteenth century, as Sennett shows, the city became a more fearsome and disturbing place from which people escaped to the sanctity and safety of their own private homes where they could lock themselves away. This is the context in which the private, inward-looking nuclear family developed. Other factors such as the loss of community and neighbourliness are connected to this theme.

> *Drawing upon your own experience, give examples to support the idea of a 'loss of community and neighbourliness'. Can you think of any examples that argue against this notion?*

Some criticisms of conventional historical approaches

Ferdinand Mount, a conservative historian and once an advisor to the former British Prime Minister Margaret Thatcher, takes issue with a number of the writers whose work has been covered in this chapter. As well as pointing to the flimsy nature of some of the historical evidence provided by historians such as Shorter, he also criticizes their work for its essentially political nature (Mount 1982).

This raises questions of values that have been a central debate within sociology as a discipline from its earliest origins. Mount claims that historians of the family have worked from a value or political position that has pictured the modern twentieth-century family – the monogamous, nuclear household of parents and children – as a recent development. Thus, as we have seen, Aries, Shorter and Stone have variously pointed to categories such as:

- romantic love,

- childhood,

- parenthood, and

- the privatized nuclear family household

as modern social constructs that are relatively new and did not exist in the same forms in the past. Such categories can be variously identified as repressive or positive depending on the value position taken. Critics stress the repressive aspects of the modern family; for instance, feminists highlight the exploitation of women that parenthood involves.

Why is parenthood exploitative of women? (This will be explored further in Chapter 5, but make an attempt to provide your own answer now.)

Take each of the other categories listed above, and explain why it could be seen as repressive.

Work in pairs or on your own and report back and/or write down your answers.

Mount's criticisms of the historical evidence used by those who portray the nuclear family as repressive can be summarized as follows:

- Questionable sources: the evidence is based on the reports of priests and doctors.

- Unrepresentative samples: the data are drawn from dominant groups or literate sections of society.

- Unreliable data: arguments resting upon stories and folk sayings such as 'Cattle are worth more than a wife' are as dubious as basing one's view of the modern family on a comedian's mother-in-law jokes.

Work in pairs, small groups or on your own to complete these exercises:

1 List some reasons why the testimony of priests and doctors may be questionable.

2 Discuss how important it is to ensure that research samples are representative.

3 Consider whether jokes and folk wisdom can accurately portray the reality of family life. Write down some suitable jokes, sayings and proverbs as evidence for or against Mount's argument.

The evidence used by the historians Mount is criticizing tends to reinforce the view that families and households were in the past in some sense better than the self-centred isolated nuclear family of today. Such approaches are to some extent harking back to a 'Golden Age' when people supposedly lived in much more harmonious, open, community-based relationships rooted in socialist-type values of caring and sharing for large groups of people. Mount doubts this, and suggests that in all probability family life – meaning a social unit in which parents and children are the central focus – has not changed much throughout history.

However, Morgan (1985) points out that the evidence Mount uses to support his position can be criticized for the same reasons that he criticizes others:

- He uses similar source material, which is unrepresentative.

- He also refers to the lives of a literate elite, which is unrepresentative.

It must also be noted that there is some concurrence between Mount's views and those of Laslett, although Laslett focuses more on nuclear households rather than nuclear families.

Summary

This chapter has examined some of the more important contributions from historians to our understanding of families and households in the past. They are important in that they have raised questions about the validity of the simple 'before' and 'after' account of family structure evolving from the extended to the nuclear type under the impact of industrialization.

They have also begun to open discussion about:

- the timing and nature of the Industrial Revolution,
- the process of industrialization, and
- the process of urbanization,

and their effects on families and households.

Historians are not in common agreement as to the nature and circumstances of such processes, so the traditional sociological view of the family evolving in a linear way in parallel with the process of industrialization is called into question.

Detailed study of the circumstances of people's lives in the past has revealed social relationships in family, kin and household groupings that were often complex and diverse. As later sections of this book will show, this is not unlike the picture of family and household lives that we can discern in the modern era.

Bibliography and further reading

Anderson, M. (1980) *Approaches to the History of the Western Family, 1500–1914*, London: Macmillan

— (1981) *Family Structure in Nineteenth Century Lancashire*, Cambridge: Cambridge University Press

Aries, P. (1960) *Centuries of Childhood*, 1973 edn, Harmondsworth: Penguin

Berger, J. (1972) *Ways of Seeing*, Harmondsworth: Penguin

Dennis, N., Henriques, F. and Slaughter, C. (1956) *Coal is Our Life*, London: Eyre & Spottiswoode

Hareven, T.K. (1994) 'Recent research on the history of the family', in M. Drake (ed.) *Time, Family and Community*, Oxford: Blackwell

Ladurie, E. Le Roy (1990) *Montaillou*, Harmondsworth: Penguin

Laslett, P. (ed.) (1972) *Household and Family in Past Time*, Cambridge: Cambridge University Press

— (1977) *Family Life and Illicit Love in Earlier Generations*, Cambridge: Cambridge University Press

— (1979) *The World We Have Lost*, London: Methuen

Morgan, D.H.J. (1985) *The Family, Politics and Social Theory*, London: Routledge

Mount, F. (1982) *The Subversive Family*, London: Jonathan Cape

Parsons, T. and Bales, E.F. (1954) *Family*, Glencoe, Illinois: Free Press

Sennett, R. (1993) *The Fall of Public Man*, London: Faber & Faber

Shorter, E. (1976) *The Making of the Modern Family*, London: Collins

Sorokin, P.I. (1959) *Cultural and Social Mobility*, Glencoe, Illinois: Free Press

Stone, L. (1990) *The Family, Sex and Marriage in England, 1500–1800*, Harmondsworth: Penguin

Tunstall, J. (1962) *The Fishermen*, London: McGibbon & Kee

Wirth, L. (1938) 'Urbanism as a way of life', *American Journal of Sociology*, Vol. 44

Young, M. and Wilmott, P. (1965) *Family and Kinship in East London*, Harmondsworth: Penguin

Essay questions

'Thus to ask what effect industrialization had on "the family" is to ignore the variability of both industrialization and families' (Diana Gittins). Discuss.

Coursework suggestions

1 Make brief notes on each of the key ideas and key contributors listed at the beginning of this chapter for your file in the section on historical approaches. Conduct the same exercise for each of the following chapters as you work through them.

2 Use the library to research and find out as much as possible about families and households in the past, following up the work of the historians discussed in this chapter. Make notes and summarize the range of your findings. Collect illustrations, old pictures and photographs similar to those used in this chapter to support your findings.

3 Use your findings as preparation for an oral history project. Interview older people, perhaps your relatives, about family lives earlier in this century. Tape recording or even camcorder filming would be useful, or make detailed notes of what is said. Then write up your findings, taking care to incorporate an evaluation of your methods of research as well as details and an assessment of your findings.

Stimulus – response questions

Item A

It is widely believed among sociology students that in the period before the Industrial Revolution, the dominant form of family life was the extended family. Michael Anderson traced this back to the work of the nineteenth-century French sociologist, Fréderic Le Play. Le Play describes a model of a stem family which was common in rural areas of Europe. The family was strongly patriarchal. The eldest son assumed the family responsibilities when his father became too old or died. The household was usually limited to the patriarch and his wife, one married son and his family, and any other unmarried children of the head of household. Such a family might have up to eighteen members. This stem family is the basis for the belief in a stable self-sufficient extended family.

Source: adapted from A. Wilson, *Family*, London: Tavistock, 1985.

Item B

Industrialization brought with it an increasing degree of geographical and occupational movement, and an increased degree of social mobility (i.e. movement between social classes, and changes of social status between the generations). Geographical and occupational movement was made possible by the mechanized modes of transport and communication during the nineteenth century, and the increased availability of means of transport – the motor-bus, the motorcar, the motorcycle, and the bicycle – during the twentieth century. These latter developments in transport largely promoted the growth of suburbs, since people could now live at greater distances from their work. It seems plausible to maintain, despite some criticisms of this view, that these forces must have had the effect of loosening the ties between the individual family and its wider kinship relationships, and diminishing the degree of social life which the family shared with groups of wider kindred. The family would no longer live within a particular locality and within a stable and wide network of kinship relationships to the same extent that it did before industrialization.

Source: R. Fletcher, *The Family and Marriage in Britain*, Harmondsworth: Penguin, 1973.

Item C

Michael Anderson's own research into the effects of industrialization on families does not, however, support the view that during industrialization extended families began to disappear.

Using data from the 1851 census of Preston, Michael Anderson found that some 23 per cent of households contained kin other than the nuclear family, a large increase over Laslett's figures and those for today. The bulk of this 'co-residence' occurred among the poor. Anderson argues that co-residence occurs when the parties involved receive net gains from the arrangement. . . .

Anderson's study of Preston indicates that, in the mid-nineteenth century, the working-class family functioned as a mutual aid organization. It provided an insurance policy against hardship and crisis. This function encouraged the extension of kinship bonds beyond the nuclear family. Such links would be retained as long as they provided net gains to those involved. Anderson concludes that the early stages of industrialization increased rather than decreased the extension of the working-class family.

Source: M. Haralambos and M. Holborn, *Sociology: Themes and Perspectives,* 4th edn, London: Collins Educational, 1995.

Item D

One of the foremost sources of data on kinship in pre-industrial Europe is the work of the Cambridge Group for the History of Population and Social Structure, of whom Peter Laslett is a prominent representative. Laslett and his associates emphasize the use of quantitative data in the historical study of the family, and one of their primary sources of data is the quasi-censuses, or listings of inhabitants in communities, compiled in periods ranging from the sixteenth to the nineteenth centuries. After examining the data for one hundred English communities, Laslett launched a profound attack on the view that industrialization brought about a decrease in the average family size.

During the period surveyed, his data suggest, average household size in the communities analysed stayed fairly constant at approximately 4.75 persons per household.

Source: adapted from T. Bilton *et al., Introductory Sociology,* 2nd edn, London: Macmillan, 1987.

(a) What is meant by the term 'extended family' (Item A, line 3)? **(1 mark)**

(b) Identify the main factors given by the author of Item B to explain the loosening of family ties. **(5 marks)**

(c) Explain in your own words the meaning of the term 'co-residence' (Item C, line 9) **(2 marks)**

(d) Using the information form the Items and elsewhere, discuss the problems sociologists face in using historical data to study family structure. **(7 marks)**

(e) Assess the evidence and arguments for and against the view that 'industrialization brought about a decrease in average family size' (Item D, lines 14–15). **(10 marks)**

3 Functionalist approaches to the family

Key ideas

- The 'march of progress' theory
- Social evolution
- The universality of the family
- The changing functions of the family
- The family as a 'haven in a heartless world'
- The 'fit' between the family and the needs of an advanced industrial society

Key contributors

- Emile Durkheim
- Herbert Spencer
- George Murdock
- Talcott Parsons
- Ronald Fletcher
- William J. Goode
- Ezra F. Vogel and Norman W. Bell

Of all the sociological perspectives on the family it could be argued that the functionalist approach presents the most positive view. Functionalist theory compares society to a biological organism, and emphasizes the order and stability that are key features of a successful society. In this approach the family – in particular the nuclear family – is seen as the key social unit and the main institution in society.

The roots of functionalism

The development of the functionalist approach in sociology has been linked with the discipline of anthropology, which is the study of small-scale, non-industrial, tribal societies such as the Yanamamo Indians in Amazonia.

Since the nineteenth century, anthropologists have carried out detailed studies of such tribes with the aim of describing their total way of life, a method of research known as ethnography. Implicit in their work has been the idea that societies can be compared to biological organisms such as the human body. In the twentieth century

Figure 3.1 The analogy between the human body and society

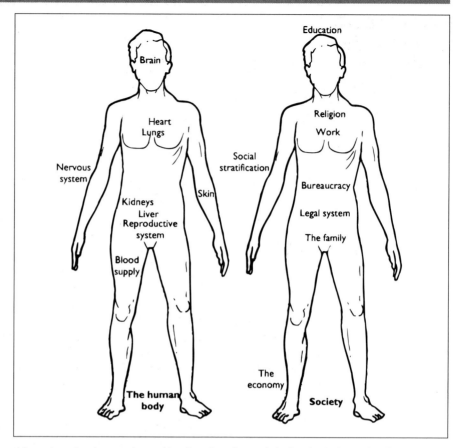

this analogy has been adopted by functionalist sociologists in their study of industrial societies.

Human bodies are composed of organs and related parts such as the heart, the brain, the skeleton, the nervous system, the blood supply and so on, each interdependent and interconnected. Society can be seen in a similar way, but society's 'components' are social institutions such as the family, education, social stratification, religion, the economic system, and so on.

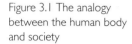 *Identify as many of society's main institutions as possible, and briefly summarize their role or function and their connections with other institutions. Draw a diagram to represent the interconnections between them.*

Note that the term 'function' is used in mathematics. 'X is a function of Y' means there is a relationship or interdependence between the two such that an alteration in the value of X also affects Y. Think of this in connection with the constituent parts of the human body and the institutions of society.

The organic analogy incorporates the idea of a system to emphasize the interrelatedness and mutual dependency of the major institutions of society. Let us consider a simple illustration. A pebble thrown into a pond causes ripples that can affect the whole pond as a 'system'. Fish and marine life are disturbed, but after a time things settle down and the pond reverts to its former calm state.

Note that the pond in its new calm state has not been dramatically altered by the

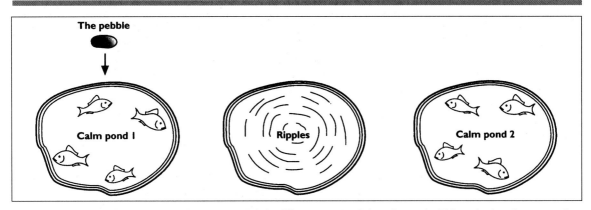

Figure 3.2 The analogy of
the pebble in a pond

pebble, but it is a slightly different 'system' than formerly. This point is relevant to the way functionalist sociologists explain change in society, as we shall discuss in more detail below (page 30).

A more complex example in relation to the human body as a 'system' would be to consider the effect of the transplant of a major organ such as the heart. What happens to the bodily 'system' after the operation? There is a crucial period of adaptation, and a vital determinant of the transplant patient's survival is whether the new heart is accepted by the body as a whole. If the new organ is rejected by the host body, other vital organs such as the kidneys, liver and lungs will fail and the patient will die. Obviously everyone concerned hopes that this will not happen and that the patient, like the pond in our earlier example, will eventually recover and return to a healthy, 'calm' state.

This 'systems approach' has been used by functionalist sociologists to explain how social change occurs in society. Functionalists see the family as the basic and most vital institution in society, just as one could see the heart and the brain as the most vital organs of the body.

Figure 3.3 Population of
working age by sex and
economic status, 1981,
1986, 1992

Source: Employment Department

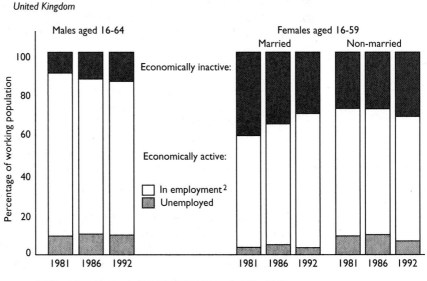

1 UK labour force definitions for 1981, ILO/OECD definitions for 1986 and 1992.

2 Includes those on government schemes for 1986 and 1992. In 1992, unpaid family workers are also included.

Source: Employment Department

Take a look at Figure 3.3, which summarizes a change that has occurred in British society in recent years.

1 What has happened to the proportion of wives going out to paid employment?

2 What effects has this change had on society and, more specifically, on family life? Have relationships within the family altered in any significant way?

Some sociologists have argued that relations between husbands and wives have altered as a result of the increase in wives' employment and that childcare has increasingly become a shared activity. Concepts such as joint conjugal roles (Bott 1971) and the symmetrical family (Young and Wilmott 1975 – see page 67) have been used to describe this new situation.

In this view family life is seen as a partnership, with parents and children all participating in household tasks such as washing up, cleaning and so on, either because this is seen as fairer than leaving all these chores for the working wife and mother or because it is in the interests of the whole family to have the income from paid female work.

This view of shared domestic work is controversial, and is examined in more detail in Chapter 5, in the section dealing with the debate about the domestic division of labour.

How do your own experiences of your family compare to the view presented above? If your own mother does not go out to work, find a partner whose mother does; compare experiences and write a brief report (up to a side of A4) to give as an oral presentation to your class.

Figure 3.4 The ripple effect on the family of an increase in working women

Functionalist sociologists would say that the effect of increasing numbers of working wives and mothers (the pebble in the pond) has been to cause changes in family life (ripples). A new situation has come about, in which activities in the home are shared, so society has entered a new stable state (the calm pond).

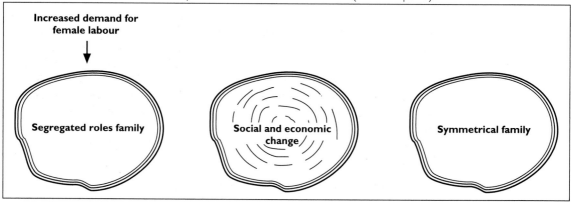

Increased demand for female labour

Segregated roles family

Social and economic change

Symmetrical family

This sort of analysis, with its emphasis on stability and equilibrium within society, has been criticized by non-functionalist sociologists.

Using the theory sections in your textbook and other sources, plus your own insights, make notes on what these criticisms might be.

Functionalists such as Robert Merton (1968) and Talcott Parsons (1959) have used concepts such as 'latent functions' and 'dysfunctions' to answer such criticisms concerning the inability of functionalism to explain social change satisfactorily.

If possible, work in pairs or groups of three. Choose another change in family life in recent times (for instance, rising unemployment among young people) and analyse this change from a functionalist perspective. Write up your account and report it to other members of your class.

The evolutionary theory

This view, also known as the 'march of progress' theory, is associated with functionalist approaches to the family. Its origins can be traced back to early sociologists such as Emile Durkheim (1858–1917) and the philosopher Herbert Spencer (1820–1903).

Durkheim (1893) presented an evolutionary view of the development of industrial society from earlier forms. He described pre-industrial societies of the past in terms of their social organization, division of labour and social solidarity, which were in essence simple in form, and showed how the process of industrialization had led to the development of more complex forms.

Figure 3.5 Durkheim's view of evolving society

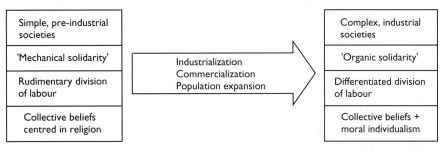

Although Durkheim did not write in detail on the family as such, his views on social solidarity, the division of labour, etc., would imply the evolution of a newer family structure – the nuclear family.

Another nineteenth-century thinker who presented an evolutionary view of societal development was the British philosopher, Herbert Spencer. Spencer has been described as a 'social Darwinist' because he applied Darwin's idea of 'the survival of the fittest' to societies. Social evolution, according to this view, involves not only social change but also the improvement and strengthening of societies, in the same way that Charles Darwin described the evolution of animal species. Just as the dinosaurs became extinct because of their evolutionary weaknesses, so 'weaker' societies that do not adapt and change will disappear and be replaced or overtaken by 'stronger' societies.

In today's terms Spencer would be regarded as a conservative or right-wing thinker, promoting pro-capitalist values. His views imply that capitalism has survived because of its inherent strengths compared to other forms of society such as feudalism.

In the mid-twentieth century, proponents of modernization theory echoed Spencer's approach with their suggestion that underdeveloped Third World societies would and should evolve through the process of industrialization to become advanced

Figure 3.6 The evolution of society: survival of the fittest?

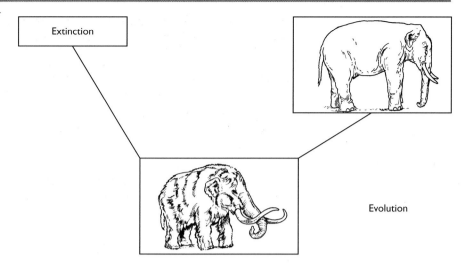

Extinction

Evolution

industrial states like the USA. More recent defenders of the capitalist system, such as the British Conservative government from 1979, would also support this view.

The evolutionary approach and the family

Tied in with the evolutionary view of societal development is the belief that societies' institutions such as the family also evolve. Functionalist sociologists say that the modern nuclear family has evolved from earlier forms and is the structure most appropriate for and beneficial to the needs of an advanced industrial society.

Figure 3.7 The evolution of the nuclear family

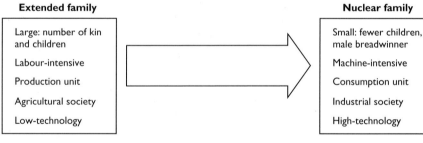

Extended family

Large: number of kin and children

Labour-intensive

Production unit

Agricultural society

Low-technology

Nuclear family

Small: fewer children, male breadwinner

Machine-intensive

Consumption unit

Industrial society

High-technology

The argument goes that in pre-industrial societies the family was of the extended type, with several generations living in a household or a close geographical area. The extended family was 'functional' in such societies because agricultural production prior to mechanization was labour intensive, so all family members could contribute to the growing of crops, care of animals, etc. Knowledge – of how to sow crops, plough, harvest, hunt, handle animals and so on – was passed down through the generations, and younger family members cared for the elderly.

 Consult some historical sources and write up to a side of A4 giving more detail on how the pre-industrial extended family shared tasks and supported all its members.

Industrialization was a long and complex process that did not take place, as the term 'Industrial Revolution' implies, over a short period. Its effects were spasmodic throughout Britain and Europe, with rapid advances in some regions while others were little affected and remained largely agricultural. This unevenness continues into the present day, and the diversity of family structures could be seen as a reflection of this variability; thus the extended family remains important in farming communities.

Societal evolution, then, involves changes in social institutions, including the family. Changes in one institution are also connected with the development or modification of others. The 'function' of transmitting knowledge from the older to the younger generation was transferred in industrial societies to agencies outside the family such as schools, colleges and universities.

 Briefly explain why this change occurs.

In a similar way, religion changes from a small-scale tribal activity within a community such as a village to a large, eventually international organizational activity, such as Catholicism, Islam, Hinduism.

Something to note with the evolutionary model is that most institutions have grown in scale and size and could increasingly be described – as pointed out by Weber – as bureaucratic, but this seems not to have happened to the family, which has apparently become smaller as the nuclear family has become predominant.

The small size and narrow range of the modern family unit has been seen by some as the perfect 'counterbalance' to the increasing impersonality and large scale of the organizations where people work, are educated, recover from illness (hospitals), shop (super/hypermarkets) and so on. It is in the family that we can 'find' ourselves. The family has been described as a 'haven in a heartless world'. This is sometimes known as the 'warm bath' theory of the family (see page 36)

Make notes to summarize and evaluate this view. Later, when you have worked through the chapters on divorce, feminist approaches, radical psychiatry, etc., you could draw on these notes to write an extended essay on the role of the family as a refuge from an impersonal world.

The nuclear family evolved, according to the functionalist perspective, because it is best suited to an industrial society: its smallness of scale makes for ease of geographical and social mobility, and it provides a haven for its members. It fits the needs of an advanced society in the same way that the larger extended family fitted the needs of an agricultural society.

Figure 3.8 Changing functions of the family

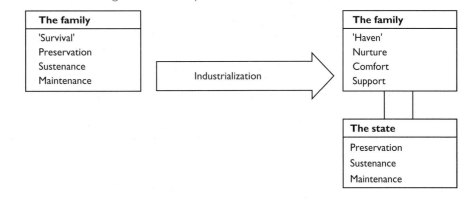

A number of criticisms have been levelled at this account. One concerns the use of the term 'function', which at its simplest implies that any existing institution and its structure are the most beneficial possible for the wider society. There is no room for alternative structures or institutions. This has been picked up by the British sociologist David Morgan, who has charged that prominent functionalists such as Talcott Parsons have not adequately considered alternatives to the nuclear family, such as communes and collective childrearing (Morgan 1973).

These issues will be reconsidered in later chapters of this book when we examine alternatives to the family and the controversy over single-parent families. For the present we shall review the work of some of the main proponents of the functionalist view of the family.

The work of Talcott Parsons

Talcott Parsons (1902–79) is regarded as the key contributor to functionalist views on the family in the twentieth century. As well as being associated with the march of progress and evolutionary approaches, his work has also been linked to the notion that the functions of the family have changed with the progress of industrialization.

In simple terms, Parsons presents us with a modern, stripped-down family structure, appropriate for an advanced industrial society such as the USA. As societies advance and industrialize, the family correspondingly adapts and evolves. In the past there was strong emphasis on the economic and maintenance needs of family members. As societies industrialize and become more complex, with an increasing division of labour and specialization of tasks, so agencies outside the family have taken over some of its responsibilities, a good example being the education of the young. Welfare benefits for the elderly, the sick and the unemployed have supplanted the economic and maintenance functions of the family.

This explanation can be linked to a set of associated ideas about change in society. Some of these have already been mentioned: the growth of bureaucracy and the increased scale and impersonality of institutions, contrasted with the closeness and intimacy of the small-scale nuclear family. Here the individual is presented as existing in a bewildering, frightening, hostile world, the damaging effects of which can be counteracted within the family.

 Why is the modern family structure nuclear rather than extended? Brainstorm in a small group to see what explanations you can come up with before you proceed to the next section.

Functionalist sociologists such as Parsons point out that modern industrial societies need a geographically and socially mobile working population. Work and occupational structures in such societies alter rapidly with changing technology, so that upward social mobility tends to occur between the generations.

To test this theory out, consider which occupation you eventually want to enter. What would this mean for your own social position compared to your parents' occupations? What about your grandparents' work? Do you find evidence of upward mobility?

The pattern in the post-war period was for the sons and daughters of those in traditional manual working-class occupations to enter more middle-class, white-collar work such as teaching, medicine, banking, law and similar service occupations. So in a social sense the younger generation could be seen as drifting apart from the older generation, thus loosening the ties with the extended family and making the nuclear family of parents and offspring more of a focal unit. Higher incomes and raised living standards mean that there is less necessity for the financial support of older relatives.

> *Three actors are required for the following role play exercise:*
>   *Write a short sketch to illustrate the social awkwardness or distance that has developed between the generations. One character is a Professor of Sociology who is visiting home. The other characters are her mother who is a cleaner in a local school and her father who is a taxi driver.*

Similarly, according to Parsons, there is a need for the family to be geographically mobile. He was writing in the context of a large country like the USA where the average family might move long distances during the working lifetime of its main breadwinner as he seeks promotion and improved job opportunities. (Note that in Parsons's work, set in 1950s' America, the husband/father is the 'natural' breadwinner.) This would clearly be problematic if an extended family of several generations was involved.

As well as challenging the somewhat dated notion of fathers as sole breadwinners, critics such as Morgan (1973) have pointed to the apparent classlessness of such families (who were in fact middle class), their lack of declared ethnic identity (in fact they were white) and similar sociological failings. The functionalist picture of a male breadwinner in a white, middle-class family does not do justice to the variety, class and ethnic differences in family structures. In the British context the persistence of extended family forms in traditional communities and among ethnic minority groups can also be seen as a challenge to the functionalist model.

> *Investigate among your friends, family and student peers whether the extended family has largely disappeared. You may need to be flexible in your definition, including family groups whose members live close to rather than with each other, to provide a realistic answer to this question.*

The changing functions of the family

For Parsons the functions of the modern family have been reduced in number over time. As discussed above, there has been a shift from the family primarily providing for the economic and maintenance needs of its members to providing emotional and related support. Two major functions remain: the socialization of children and the stabilization of the adult personality.

The primary socialization of children

This concerns the way children are brought up by parents in accordance with prevailing norms and values. They learn from parents how to 'fit' into society, to distinguish between right and wrong, and so on.

> *Think of examples of parent–child interactions that illustrate this function.*

The stabilization of adult personality

This refers to the notion of the family as a haven in a heartless world referred to earlier. The nuclear family provides social stability for its members that is necessary in a world where outside life can be pressurized, chaotic and highly impersonal.

Note that this particularly applies to the male breadwinner because, as we have noted, Parsons identified a 'natural' division of labour in which the husband goes out to work in the rational, impersonal domain to earn money for the family, while the wife stays at home and plays an expressive, emotionally supportive role that Parsons felt was a reflection of a biological difference between the sexes.

This is the 'warm bath' theory: the husband arrives home from a stressful day at work and sinks into the 'warm bath' that his family provides. In line with this theory, a recent television documentary featured a father of young children who described his small children greeting him at the door after a hectic day at work as putting everything into perspective and making his life seem worthwhile.

Figure 3.9 Warm bath theory

To summarize, Parsons presents a model of the family that has been stripped of its earlier functions and has evolved into a small social unit that provides its members with comfort and security in an increasingly bureaucratic and impersonal world. This also 'fits' the needs of an advanced society because the small, flexible family can move geographically and socially with little hindrance from large kinship networks.

William J. Goode

William J. Goode added to the functionalist view in a study of family trends throughout the world entitled *World Revolution and Family Patterns* (Goode 1963).

His basic thesis was that there is a worldwide trend towards a monogamous nuclear family structure. In response to claims that there is a diversity of family forms in the world including polygamy, clan and extended families, social rather than biological fatherhood, ghost weddings and so on, Goode argued that there was a universal trend towards the Western model of the nuclear family because, like Parsons, he saw this as an integral part of the global expansion of industrialization.

> *Do you agree that the world is becoming industrialized in the way suggested by 'march of progress' theorists? Could it be that this view is outdated? Discuss the issues with your teachers/tutors, and consult suitable library sources. Make a link with themes from the sociology of development, Third World studies, etc.*

Goode's argument could be updated with reference to the global expansion of dominant Western forms of culture (literature, mass media), spreading images of the ideals of romantic love and nuclear family life, which thus become desirable to increasing numbers of people across the world. Thus in countries where polygamy (usually polygyny) has traditionally been permitted, economic development has been accompanied by a tendency to see the practice as outmoded, and more Westernized forms of family structure have become increasingly popular.

 This development may to some extent be welcomed by feminists, who would see polygyny as a more oppressive social relationship for women than the Western nuclear family. Do some research on polygyny, and explain why this may be so.

George Peter Murdock

Murdock was one of the first to apply a functionalist approach to the family. He investigated societies throughout the world and concluded that the family is a universal institution. This immediately raises the question: what is meant by the family in this context? According to Murdock's definition:

> The family is a social group characterized by common residence, economic co-operation and reproduction. It includes adults of both sexes, at least two of whom maintain a socially approved sexual relationship, and one or more children, own or adopted, of the sexually co-habiting adult.
>
> (Murdock 1949)

In pairs or small groups, or on your own, examine this definition and draw up a list of the various family types it might describe.

In practice, despite the very open-ended definition we have quoted, Murdock, like other evolutionary theorists such as Parsons and Goode, focused on the development throughout the world of the nuclear family.

Ronald Fletcher

Ronald Fletcher, a British sociologist who wrote on the family in the post-war period, offered a functionalist analysis that was somewhat at odds with Parsons's view that the functions of the family have been reduced in the twentieth century. Fletcher suggested that, if anything, the modern family has an increased number of functions, as follows:

- regulating sexual behaviour;

- providing a responsible basis for procreation and the rearing of children;

- caring for dependent members, whether young or old;

- acting as the earliest and most powerful socializing agency;

- teaching family members the roles they will play in society, and helping them to accept the rights, duties and obligations linked to those roles.

In his study of the British family Fletcher (1966) emphasized the strength of this family structure.

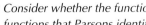 *Consider whether the functions listed above can be reconciled with the two functions that Parsons identified for the modern family.*

Ezra F. Vogel and Norman W. Bell

Vogel and Bell (1968) focused on the dysfunctions of family life that produce emotionally disturbed children. An example is the scapegoating of a child for conflicts that in reality are occurring between a husband and wife. The family remains intact, despite the suffering caused to the child, so Vogel and Bell drew the somewhat uncomfortable conclusion that the survival of the family unit may demand the sacrifice of a child's happiness or mental stability.

This is an interesting argument that may highlight a weakness in the functionalists' case. Everything within the family and other social institutions is seen in terms of its functions. Functionalism is thus teleological: it holds that society, its institutions and social relationships can always be seen as moving towards some end state. So emotional disturbance in a child has the function of preserving the satisfactory (for whom?) end state of an intact family. We can take the argument a stage further by imagining that the emotionally disturbed child has to be cared for by social workers, child psychiatrists and so on. This is also presumably 'functional' for society as it provides work for such professionals. Indeed, 'functions' can be found for almost any feature of family life, good or bad, as critics of functionalism point out.

Select another example of a 'dysfunction' like Vogel and Bell's, and show how it can be explained within a functionalist approach.

Functionalism and the New Right

The functionalist approach is most often to be found in the work of American sociologists such as Parsons, with their emphasis on the white, middle-class family that might have existed in the USA in the 1940s and 1950s.

However, functionalism has been brought into the 1990s by New Right thinkers and writers (see Chapter 8). They argue for a return to an idealized strong nuclear family closely related to the original functionalist model. Their view could be summed up in the statement: 'Every family should comprise two loving married parents raising their own children.'

Discuss in pairs, or make notes on, the difficulty of reconciling this political objective with the reality of family life for many people.

Somewhat at odds with the functionalist approach, the New Right use deviations from this model (in particular the one-parent family) to attack what they identify as worrying trends in society – rising divorce rates, fatherless families, social disorder, rising crime and related social 'ills'. In a sense the New Right wants to turn the clock back to a 'Golden Age' when the functionalist model of the family was predominant. In later sections of this book we shall be questioning whether such a family, based on a male breadwinner and his dependent wife and children, has ever been the experience for the majority of people.

Conclusion

Functionalists present a strongly positive view of a particular family structure – the nuclear family. They stress how well this type of family 'fits' the needs of an advanced industrial society, and maintain that the evolutionary nature of its development underlines its efficiency as well as its implied desirability. Later sections of this book will examine the support for this view.

Household occupancy statistics (see pages 155–6) show that most people spend a significant proportion of their lives in a form of nuclear family. Despite high divorce rates in many countries of the world, most marriages remain intact and the majority of children live with, and are raised to adulthood, by both their parents.

Critics point to weaknesses of the functionalist argument, for instance its assumption that it brings benefits to *all* family members. Feminists ask how the family can be described as benefiting women when, in their view, it is a major source of female oppression. The high proportion of working wives and mothers, particularly since the 1960s, is also not easily accommodated within the traditional functionalist model. The rising level of cohabitation and the breakdown of marriage have convinced others that the family is becoming increasingly diverse and is not evolving towards some unitary structure as represented by writers such as Goode. More theoretical criticisms concern the constant emphasis on how institutions such as the family can be seen in terms of their function or purpose for the 'benefit' of society.

However, despite such criticisms, the functionalist approach to the family must be considered seriously, and it is still a powerful force in sociological and wider political debates about the desirability of nuclear families for social stability and well-being generally.

Bibliography and further reading

Bell, N.W. and Vogel, E.F. (1968) *A Modern Introduction to the Family*, New York: Free Press

Bott, E. (1971) *Family and Social Network*, 2nd edn, London: Tavistock

Durkheim, E. (1960) *The Division of Labour in Society*, (1893), New York: Free Press

Fletcher, R. (1966) *The Family and Marriage in Britain*, Harmondsworth: Penguin

Goode, W.J. (1963) *World Revolution and Family Patterns*, New York: Free Press

Merton, R.K. (1968) *Social Theory and Social Structure*, enlarged edn, New York: Free Press

Morgan, D. (1973) *Social Theory and the Family*, London: Routledge & Kegan Paul

Murdock, G. (1949) *Social Structure*, London: Macmillan

Parsons, T. (1959) 'The social structure of the family', in R.N. Anshen (ed.) *The Family: Its Functions and Destiny*, New York: Harper & Row

— 'The normal American family', in S.M. Farber (ed.) *Man and Civilization: The Family's Search for Survival*, New York: McGraw-Hill

Vogel, E.F. and Bell, N.W. (1968) 'The emotionally disturbed child as the family scapegoat', in N.W. Bell and E.F. Vogel (eds) *A Modern Introduction to the Family*, rev. edn, New York: Free Press

Young, M. and Wilmott, P. (1975) *The Symmetrical Family*, Harmondsworth: Penguin

Essay questions

Write 1,200–1,500 words on the following topics:

1 'Functionalist accounts of the family underestimate the extent of strain and exploitation in family life.' Discuss.

2 Examine the view that there is a global trend towards a predominantly nuclear family structure.

3 'The nuclear family "fits" the needs of an advanced industrial society.' Discuss.

Coursework suggestions

Look again at some of the activities in this chapter. Do any of them give you ideas about a more detailed study that could become a coursework project of up to 5,000 words in length?

You could, for instance, investigate in detail whether the functionalist approach presents a satisfactory account of family life in your own society by carrying out an investigation among friends, fellow students, neighbours and relatives. Which methods of research would be most appropriate for such a topic?

Stimulus – response questions

(for AEB candidates)

Item A

The nuclear family was a nest. Warm and sheltering, it kept the children secure from the pressure of the outside adult world, and gave the men an evening refuge from the icy blast of competition. And as the nuclear family rose in the nineteenth century, the women liked it too, because it let them pull back from the grinding exactions of farm work, or the place at the mill, and devote themselves to child care. So everyone huddled happily within those secure walls, serene about the dinner table, united in the Sunday outing.

Source: E. Shorter, *The Making of the Modern Family*, London: Fontana, 1977.

Item B

The husband, by virtue of his greater participation in the external economic division of labour compared to his wife, was able legitimately to avoid many household tasks and legitimately to dominate family life. To paraphrase Engels, the fact that not all husbands used their power does not in the least change the position of wives. The wife, by virtue of her relative exclusion from paid work and her major responsibility for the home and the children, was consigned to economic and social dependence upon her husband.

In contrast to certain optimistic theorists who claim that the nineteenth-century patriarchal family has been superseded by a more democratic type, the present study provides abundant evidence of the survival of patriarchalism.

Source: adapted from S. Edgell, *Middle-class Couples*, London: George Allen & Unwin, 1980.

Item C

As nuclear families become more isolated, the network of kinsfolk becomes dispersed. The young mother can still talk to her mum on the telephone, but she can't ask her to drop in for a few minutes to mind the baby. Ideas about the status of women have been changing; wives are now thought of as companions rather than servants to their husbands, but perhaps they are even more thoroughly enslaved to their children than before.

Source: E. Leach, 'The family as an instrument of women's enslavement', *Sunday Times Magazine*, 10 November 1986.

Item D

The family-household system of contemporary capitalism constitutes not only the central site of the oppression of women but an important organizing principle of the relations of production and the social formation as a whole. This is not necessarily inevitable, since the argument that it would not be possible for capitalism's relations of production to be organized in other ways has yet to be proven. Furthermore, it is evident that the contemporary family-household system has incorporated a substantial element from struggles between the interests of men and those of women, by and large in favour of the former. However, it still remains the case that the specific combination of gender and class relations that characterizes this system has entrenched the gender division in the fabric of capitalist social relations in a particularly effective way.

Source: adapted from M. Barratt, *Women's Oppression Today: Problems in Marxist Feminist Analysis*, London: Verso, 1980.

Item E

Originally, feminist research began with a commitment to exposing the oppression of women and uncovering and claiming women's experiences as valid. More recently it has concentrated on how women resist oppression. Implicit in all this is a critique of male power.

Feminists are concerned to improve the situation of women. So they conduct research which provides evidence for the need to instigate change. They disrupt prevailing notions of what is inevitable and ask what is the damage of not changing social conditions. Research on child sexual abuse, domestic violence and marital rape suggests that the longer the ideological myth of the family as a safe haven from the outside world is perpetuated, the greater will be the damage that is done to women and children

Source: adapted from B. Skeggs, 'Confessions of a feminist researcher', *Sociology Review*, September 1992.

(a) According to Item A, how is power distributed within the nuclear family?
(2 marks)

(b) Explain in your own words the meaning of the term 'patriarchalism' (Item B, line 16).
(2 marks)

(c) Using material from the Items above and elsewhere, assess the view that 'ideas about the status of women have been changing' (Item C, lines 5–6). **(7 marks)**

(d) The author of Item A argues that the family keeps 'children secure form the pressure of the outside adult world' (lines 2–3). Illustrating your answer with material from the Items above, assess the extent to which this view is supported by sociological evidence.
(5 marks)

(e) Using material from Items D, E and elsewhere, assess the view that the family in contemporary capitalist society does not serve the needs of its members. **(9 marks)**

4

Marxist and socialist-feminist approaches

'Marx and Engels may have called, in the polemical rhetoric of the Communist Manifesto, for the abolition of the family, but most socialists have long since regarded this as a flight of utopian fancy.'

(Barrett and McIntosh 1982, p. 7)

Key ideas

- Evolutionary views of the family
- Changed relationships between men and women
- Promiscuity
- Polygamy
- Monogamy
- Savagery to barbarism to civilization
- Matriarchy
- Patriarchy
- The family as an ideological state apparatus·
- The family as a 'haven in a heartless world'
- Marxism and feminism
- Socialist feminism

Key figures

- Karl Marx
- Friedrich Engels
- Lewis Henry Morgan
- Louis Althusser
- Jacques Donzelot
- Christopher Lasch
- Kathleen Gough
- Coontz and Henderson
- Michel Foucault
- Michele Barrett and Mary McIntosh
- David Lane
- Hilda Scott

In the previous chapter we examined the functionalist approach to the family, which presents a strongly positive view of the role of the nuclear family in modern society. In the following three chapters we shall be exploring theories that are critical of the stereotypical family and its effects on individual members and the wider society. The approaches we shall be considering cover a range of views and emphases, and offer different explanations of how the family is a 'harmful' institution for many people.

This chapter begins by comparing the Marxist and functionalist approaches before taking a look at the traditional Marxist account of the family that originated with the work of Friedrich Engels (1820–95), Marx's friend and collaborator. Then we shall examine some of the more modern versions of Marxism (Neo-Marxism) expressed in the work of Althusser, Donzelot and Lasch. The following section looks at recent attempts to forge links between Marxism and feminism, and finally we shall consider whether the experience of socialist societies lends support to the Marxist and socialist-feminist case.

Marxism and functionalism

Although Marxist approaches are usually seen as diametrically opposed to the functionalist view of the family, there are some points of concurrence. The two schools of thought begin by asking similar questions about the family in society:

- What is the purpose (function) of the family?

- How did the modern family originate?

- What is the relationship of the family to the wider society?

Another similarity is that in some respects Marxism can be seen to offer a somewhat puritanical view of relationships. Some Marxists criticized the hypocritical aspects of the bourgeois family under Victorian capitalism:

- the double standard applied to wives' and husbands' adultery;

- the role of mistresses;

- prostitution;

- sexual licence and experimentation for males as symptoms of the corrupt bourgeois way of life.

Under socialism, relationships based on fidelity, loyalty and openness would be favoured. These key socialist principles are very like the ideal that a monogamous loving relationship within a stereotypical nuclear family seems to encompass.

However, these similarities appear fairly minor in view of the main emphases of the two traditions. Marxists disagree with the functionalist assumption that the family benefits all members equally. Along with feminists and other critical theorists, they point out that the family:

- reflects inequalities in the wider society, especially the distinction between exploiter and exploited;

- supports capitalist values;

- exploits and oppresses some members, notably women as wives and mothers;

- is an ideological institution, since the family – particularly the stereotypical nuclear family of breadwinner husband, dependent wife and children – is presented as the 'normal' and 'natural' pattern of domestic social organization.

The family theory of Friedrich Engels

Engels' work *The Origin of the Family, Private Property and the State* was first published in 1884, a year after Marx's death. It is often seen as the first exposition of a Marxist approach to the family. Its central ideas are that there is a link between family form and private property, and that this is reinforced by legislation enacted by the state under capitalism.

It was Marx who was first impressed by a work of the American anthropologist Lewis Henry Morgan (1818–81) entitled *Ancient Society*. Engels used Marx's notes as the basis for what he originally intended to be a review pamphlet, but he eventually developed his ideas into a book.

Morgan's work seemed to provide the basis for an evolutionary explanation of the monogamous modern family rooted in an understanding of social and economic change which could be associated with the development of capitalism. His book, subtitled *Researches in the Lines of Human Progress from Savagery through Barbarism to Civilization*, attempted to construct a history of stages of social organization and of the family.

Figure 4.1 Marxist stages of history

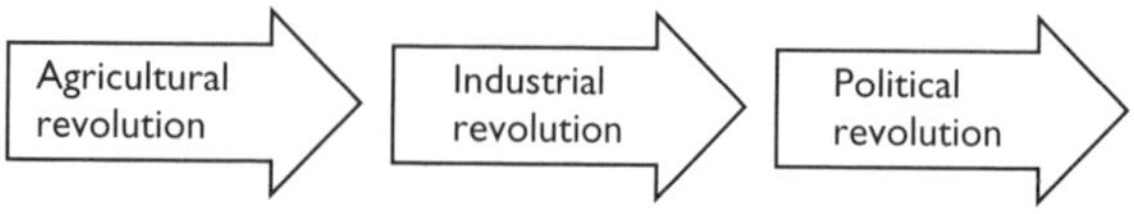

	Primitive communism	Feudalism	Capitalism	Socialism
Production	Hunter-gatherer bands	Landowners and serfs	Owners and workers	Common ownership
Stratification	Classless society	Aristocracy and peasantry	Bourgeoisie and proletariat	Classless society
Authority	Matriarchy	Patriarchy		Equality
Context of reproduction	Group marriage	Extended family	Nuclear family	Community family

Arrows above table: Agricultural revolution → Industrial revolution → Political revolution

Engels developed these themes, and his resultant book has since provided a starting point for any discussion of how Marxism, and more recently Marxist-Feminism, should analyse the relationship between the present 'bourgeois' (a Marxist term) monogamous family type and changes in society at the economic level. Figure 4.1 illustrates the theory in its simplest form.

The Marxist approach is an evolutionary one since it relates the way societies have evolved over time to the ways social relationships develop into particular types of

	Pre-historic	**Medieval**	**Industrial**
Economy	Primitive communism Hunting and gathering	Feudalism Agriculture	Capitalism Industry
Property	No ownership	Landownership	Ownership of the means of production by the bourgeoisie
Authority	Matriarchy	Patriarchy	
Context for reproduction	Group marriage No biological father identity	Extended family	Nuclear family
Inheritance	None Parental identity unimportant	Patrilineal primogeniture (property passed to first-born male heir) Parental identity increasingly important	

Figure 4.2 The evolution of society and its effects on families and households.

family. Engels' approach can be represented diagrammatically as in Figure 4.2.

> *Study Figure 4.2 closely. Is it satisfactory? What criticisms can be made of it?*

Engels makes the following key points in his account of the development of the family:

- Initially societies were 'primitive communist': there was no property ownership, and caring and sharing were performed equally. This makes sense in a subsistence society, where one person would kill an animal which all would share, and the favour would be reciprocated later when someone else made a kill.

> *In what way does the illustration of early humans in Figure 4.3 reflect the modern stereotype of the family?*

- Sexual relations were promiscuous – here Engels used Morgan's anthropological evidence for the existence of group marriages, with a number of sexual partners.

- Women were more powerful than men at this stage – society was matriarchal.

- The development of ownership of property – originally land for agriculture, later

Figure 4.3 A prehistoric 'family'

houses and factories – produced societies in which men were more powerful: patriarchal societies.

Figure 4.4 'Christmas Hamper' by Robert Braithwaite (1826–69), Courtesy of the Bridgeman Art Library

Figure 4.4 is a painting of a stereotypical Victorian extended family. How typical do you think this scene was in the nineteenth century?

- Men consolidated their dominance through the system of patrilineality – the inheritance of property through the male line, from father to son. If the eldest male is the sole heir, this system is called primogeniture.

In such societies there is a strong emphasis on the physical resemblance between a father and son. Why is this emphasis so important in a society based on patrilineal descent?

- The monogamous family developed alongside patriarchy (see above), which created dominant and powerful males and subservient females and children.

Evaluating Engels' theory

For and against the theory of primitive promiscuity

Some anthropologists, such as Kathleen Gough (1972), suggest that Engels' (and Morgan's) picture of promiscuous sexual relations in early societies was probably accurate. Gough based her view on a study of some of our nearest animal relatives – chimpanzees, who live in promiscuous tribes. However, the majority of anthropological and similar studies have raised doubts about the evidence for Engels' views on the lives of people in early societies.

Coontz and Henderson (1986) suggest that, rather than some societies being matriarchal, it was more probable that males and females were equal as such societies were based on the sharing of resources. The parenthood of children was

Figure 4.5 'Young Willy's very much like his father isn't he?' Courtesy of *Private Eye*

not important as all members of the group, tribe or clan, even strangers or outsiders, would be fed equally.

Some commentators stress the almost complete lack of evidence from twentieth-century studies to support Engels' and Morgan's case. Research has found that tribal societies can be based on monogamous relationships and forms of nuclear family in which biological parents can be identified with their children.

From a political stance it could be argued that Engels' (and Marx's) socialist beliefs, stressing the sharing of all property and economic resources on an equal basis, would be compatible with the idea of sexual 'sharing' and equality, so no one person 'owns'

Figure 4.6 Communal living in the 1960s

or 'possesses' another as in a monogamous relationship reinforced by marriage vows. Such ideas were taken up in the 1960s and 1970s by the commune movement (see Chapter 11) in Europe and the USA where people of left-wing or socialist persuasion advocated communal living and sexual sharing in promiscuous group marriages. Many of these movements were short-lived and now seem naïve, not to mention their association with drug subcultures.

Regarding the stability of such social relationships, the British sociologist Peter Worsley and others have claimed that no society based on promiscuity has ever survived for long.

Ethnocentrism

It must also be noted that Engels' and Morgan's ideas were of their time, and the terms they used – earlier societies were said to be 'barbaric' and 'savage', whereas modern societies were 'civilized' – are today considered ethnocentric (treating your own society as superior to others).

> *On your own or as a group activity, look up a more detailed definition of ethnocentrism and think of some further more modern examples in relation to the family.*

Engels' work on the family has been severely criticized, and some have argued that his views have no place in contemporary debates. In her introduction to *The Origins of the Family, Private Property and the State*, Michele Barrett summarizes feminist criticisms of Engels by pointing to his somewhat rosy notion of women's position in the past: 'It must be conceded that by the lights of contemporary feminism the equality between the sexes that is evoked is an extremely limited one.' Nevertheless Barrett feels that his work is still a useful starting point for an analysis of the family. It attempts to relate the family to wider issues,such as the economic and political structure of societies, and provides a useful springboard for socialist-related and feminist debates that are still continuing.

Neo-Marxist approaches to the family

The work of Louis Althusser

Althusser was a French Marxist closely associated with a debate among Neo-Marxists about the role of the state under capitalism. Earlier Marxist approaches suggested that the state was a capitalist state, meaning that the government and related institutions served the interests of the capitalist or ruling class. Althusser's contribution to this somewhat complex debate was an analysis of what he termed 'state apparatuses', of which he distinguished two forms:

- *Repressive state apparatuses* are the more overt or visible means of social control, such as the police, prisons and the army, which have powers to discipline and punish transgressors against the capitalist system, such as strikers imprisoned for breaking anti-strike legislation.

- *Ideological state apparatuses* control people's behaviour by more covert or abstract means such as through the manipulation of ideas and beliefs. In question here are agencies such as education and religion and in more modern contexts the mass media.

Althusser saw the family as an institution that supports capitalism in similar ways to the Church and school. As an agent of social control over its members, particularly children, it contains potential rebellion against or criticism of the capitalist status quo. For example, parents encouraging homework and doing well at school could be interpreted as passing on ideological messages about the virtues of individual hard work and competitiveness.

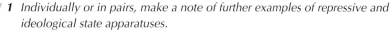

1 Individually or in pairs, make a note of further examples of repressive and ideological state apparatuses.

2 Could the family be seen as a repressive as well as an ideological state apparatus? If so, in what ways?

Neo-Marxist supporters of the family under capitalism

Althusser offers an uncompromising view of capitalist society that is strongly rooted in traditional critical approaches. However, some Marxist-influenced scholars take a different view and see the family in a more positive light.

Christopher Lasch is an American cultural critic who supports the view of the family as a haven or retreat from the harshness of the capitalist world outside (the 'warm bath' theory discussed on pages 33–6). Lasch (1977) and a French Marxist, Jacques Donzelot (1980), portray the family in the modern world as an institution under siege from various agencies of the state. A variety of experts, professionals and counsellors intervene in the secure private world of the family, effectively to control and supervise it.

1 Think of some examples of such 'experts, professionals and counsellors'. Elaborate on how such people may intervene in private family lives.

2 You could develop this exercise into a detailed discussion and examination addressing the question whether 'social workers in the twentieth century have increasingly become the professional busybodies of the state'.

3 Which social classes and groups in society are most likely to experience such 'experts', and why?

Donzelot's views are influenced by Michel Foucault (1926–84), a French thinker whose writings on power, authority and sexuality have received increasing attention from social scientists in recent years.

Foucault is not normally associated with a Marxist perspective, but his work falls clearly within the 'critical' tradition and has influenced some Marxist writers. He opposed the conventional view that over time societies have become more democratic and liberal so that the individual has become 'freer' from the state and governmental control. Foucault believed that, rather than diminishing, this 'power' has changed and evolved into new forms that are in effect just as repressive as what came before them.

To give an example, the horrific treatment of criminals in the past, which often involved torture and dismemberment, is generally seen as barbaric and uncivilized in comparison with the more 'humane' treatment of offenders today. Foucault raised doubts about this by pointing out that incarceration in cells and 24-hour surveillance of prisoners can be as bad as, if not worse than, the so-called 'barbarism' of the past.

Lasch and Donzelot apply this line of argument to the family and suggest that family life in the past was in some ways better than it is today. Their views are associated with Marxism because they are critical of the effects of capitalism in the modern world. They identify a trend towards increasing interference in and invasion of the private world of the family, an institution they see as potentially safe and secure, giving individuals opportunities for freedom and self-expression in an otherwise exploitative and repressive society. An army of professional experts is on hand to intervene in families and tell people how to run their private lives; through these experts the state acts ever more vigorously to control people.

Figure 4.7 'An army of professional experts'

In what ways do these views differ from conventional ideas about social workers and their role? Using evidence from newspaper sources (CD-ROM if available), try to construct accounts that support both views.

In the early 1990s, controversies over the Child Support Agency (see page 132) and proposed legislation to prevent parents from smacking their children could be adduced as examples of the encroachment of the state upon private lives. Lasch sees these trends as part of the decline of parental authority which has led to the growth of a pernicious self-centred individualism.

Agency 'damaging divided families'

The Child Support Agency has done nothing for children and has often worsened relations in divided families, the five leading children's charities say today.

Their claim is based on a report they commissioned to track the experiences of a sample of lone mothers towards the end of the first year of the agency's operation.

Guardian, 30 September 1994

> *Is smacking children a 'family' or parental matter? Should it be classed as 'child abuse' and become subject to 'state' control as an illegal act?*

Evaluation

Not surprisingly, the work of Lasch and Donzelot has attracted criticism, particularly from feminist writers such as Michele Barrett and Mary McIntosh who take issue with the romanticized and idealized notion of families in the past and to the implicit support for patriarchal authority.

Lasch suggests that in earlier times the family was a homogeneous institution rather close to the stereotypical nuclear family model. As we saw in Chapter 2, several historians have questioned this account, pointing to evidence of variability in family forms. Doubts have been raised about whether in pre-industrial times there even existed the concept of 'family' as we would understand it today.

Barrett and McIntosh (1982) also charge that the accounts of Lasch and Donzelot mask the inequality in their ideal households, where in reality men were authority figures and powerful, while women were oppressed and largely powerless. They criticize the sexism and anti-feminism that run through the works of these authors: Lasch typically refers only to male children, and Donzelot laments the fate of husbands who have become 'henpecked' as a result of modern trends.

Marxism and feminism

Marxist feminism focuses on the oppression of women, rooted in the family and linked to capitalism. For Marxist-feminist writers the cause of inequalities between men and women, both outside and within the family, is the economic and social structure engendered by capitalist society. Capitalism needs a cheap and easily exploitable labour force so that profits can be maximized for the ruling class – the capitalists.

Women in the family serve these interests in a number of ways:

- As mothers within families, women bear children who – if male – will become the next generation of capitalist 'wage slaves'.

- As wives, women serve and service their husbands by doing housework, cooking meals and satisfying their sexual needs. Their husbands (the wage slaves) are thereby refreshed and restored, ready to return to the world of exploitative work under capitalism.

The Marxist sociologist Eli Zaretsky (1976) has clearly articulated these views.

- As mothers, women bring up children to accept authority and be competitive; such children are socialized into the norms and values of capitalism.

This echoes the ideological aspects of the family identified by Althusser that we discussed earlier in this chapter. David Cooper (1972; and see Chapter 6) sees the family as 'an ideological conditioning device in an exploitive society'. Diane Feeley (1972) claims that the family with its 'authoritarian ideology is designed to teach passivity, not rebellion'.

- Wives are used by male wage slaves to relieve the tensions caused by their alienation under capitalism. Domestic violence against wives is sometimes the outcome (see pages 79–81).

Fran Ansley (quoted in Bernard 1976, p. 233) supports this argument when she says: 'With every worker provided with a sponge to soak up his possible revolutionary ire, the bosses rest more secure.'

- Men (husbands) can exploit their wives, despite themselves being exploited in the workplace.

- Capitalism gains from the unpaid labour of women as wives and mothers because this helps to keep wage costs down.

Some insurance companies issuing life insurance policies based on the death of a wife have costed her contribution as high as £15,000 per year.

Draw up a list of all the tasks carried out by a mother at home caring for three young children aged 5, 8 and 10 years. How many hours are involved, and what would it cost per week or year even at low wage rates of £3–4 per hour?

- The family acts to stabilize the male workforce because 'family responsibilities' could limit the desire to strike and take part in industrial action for higher wages and better working conditions.

Margaret Benston (1972) argues: 'As an economic unit, the nuclear family is a valuable stabilizing force in capitalist society. Since the production that is done in the home is paid for by the husband-father's earnings, his ability to withhold labour from the market is much reduced.'

Do you think anything is lacking from the above accounts of the way the family and women serve the interests of capitalism? Which key features of modern family life, notably the roles of wives and mothers, are omitted?

Discuss in pairs, and draw up a list of points to support your answers.

The work of Michele Barrett and Mary McIntosh

In *The Anti-Social Family* (1982) Barrett and McIntosh take a Marxist-feminist position, portraying the family as essentially an ideological instrument under capitalism. They use the concept of 'familialism', which is the ideology of the nuclear family based on a breadwinner husband and exploited dependent wife. Family life is placed on a pedestal and advocated as the natural or normal way for people to live.

They describe this as 'anti-social' because it excludes other people and relationships that do not conform to the ideal. This has the effect of making large sections of society feel inadequate or even deviant.

Lesbian couples raising children are one example of a group who are excluded from the stereotypical family norm in Barrett and McIntosh's terms.

1 Discuss in pairs or small groups or work individually to make a list of the sorts of difficulties lesbian couples can encounter.

2 Make a list of some other groups or type of households that do not conform

Court makes lesbian pair joint parents

A lesbian couple are thought to have made legal history by winning a High Court ruling making them joint parents of a 22-month-old child.

A judge in chambers granted the pair a joint residence order, giving the mother's partner equal parental responsibility for the boy. Lawyers expect the order – supported by the Official Solicitor, representing the child - to lead to similar applications.

The couple, in their 20s and from the Manchester area, decided they wanted a child shortly after they started living together. One of them made a private arrangement to become pregnant by a man who wanted no part in the child's life. No money changed hands. After the birth, the mother's partner applied for a residence order under the 1989 Children Act.

Making the order last Friday in the High Court in Manchester, Mr Justice Douglas-Brown said the child's welfare was paramount. The evidence pointed overwhelmingly in its favour.

Such an order could also be an option for lesbian couples caring for the children of one partner by a previous marriage or relationship.

Guardian, 30 June 1994

to the nuclear family stereotype and again note the difficulties they may encounter.

3 In what ways could 'familialism' be seen as equivalent to racism or sexism?

Barrett and McIntosh advocate experiments in new ways of living, and support political campaigns to transform the society that needs the family as it currently exists. Along with other Marxist-feminist writers, they offer a powerful analysis that links gender issues to the family under capitalism and highlights key features of women's role and position in society.

However, a number of criticisms have been levelled at their work:

- As with the functionalist approach, Barrett and McIntosh tend to treat the family as if it were a homogeneous unit. There is no reference to different types and variations in family life, for example between classes and over time.

- Their picture of the family as comprising a male breadwinner with dependent wife and children is now out of date, considering the proportion of wives and mothers who go out to work (see Figure 3.3 on page 29).

- They ignore current diversities in family types such as single-parent families and families in ethnic minority communities.

- Some feminists have suggested that women are very much a side issue in the 'grand Marxist' explanation of the failings of capitalism. For instance, Hartmann

Figure 4.8 Working
mothers in Britain

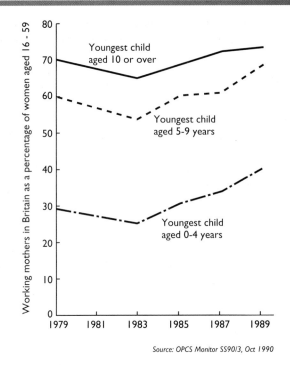

Source: OPCS Monitor SS90/3, Oct 1990

(1981) claims that, for Marxist-feminists, Marxism is the dominant focus and feminism is very much in the background.

Will women's oppression disappear under socialism?

As we have noted, Marxist feminism sees the 'problems' of women's oppression, inequality between the sexes within the family and related issues, as products of a capitalist society. The 'answer' to these 'problems', according to the Marxist-feminist model, is to overthrow capitalism and create a socialist society. In a socialist society men and women will be equal and there will be no exploitation and oppression of women. Everyone will own the 'means of production' (workplaces, factories, offices, shops) and all will share in the products of their labour.

Changes in family life and relationships between men and women are brought about by state provision of childcare and women's involvement in paid labour outside the home (which has been compulsory in some socialist societies). Despite the collapse of Communism in Eastern European societies and the break-up of the former Soviet Union, vestiges of this philosophy remain in those countries. Kindergarten and nursery care for children are provided cheaply or free for longer hours than in the West. It is possible for a parent to leave a child at nursery early in the morning and collect him or her in the evening after a full day's work.

In Britain and other Western societies childcare hours are much shorter. This restricts the working hours of many women, who are almost invariably assumed to have the main responsibility for children.

1 *Working in pairs or individually, make a list of points that explain why longer hours of nursery care in Britain could enhance women's opportunities.*

 2 *Conduct research among mothers of young children to see if they believe extra childcare hours would enhance their career and job opportunities.*

Empirical studies of the socialist states

Studies of socialist societies have not tended to lend much support to the Marxist-feminist case. David Lane's studies of the former USSR in the 1960s (Lane 1970) showed that in comparison to Westernized capitalist societies women were better represented at all levels in the workforce and that childcare provision for working parents was much better. However, closer examination of the labour force showed that inequalities between men and women still existed, and there remained some segregation of men's and women's work. While in some areas women's representation was apparently high compared to Western societies, for instance in professions such as medicine and engineering, this was not such a breakthrough as it seemed because these occupations were less well paid and carried less status than their equivalents in the West. Moreover senior managers and administrators in most occupations were predominantly male. The same applied to political institutions, where women were underrepresented in key positions of power.

In family life a similar picture of inequality emerged. If anything, because of the rural nature of large parts of the Soviet Union, attitudes to male and female domestic responsibilities were more traditional than those that prevailed in the West. 'Mother' and 'grandmother' figures dominated domestic labour and childcare. The lack of a supportive infrastructure of small businesses (considered ideologically unsound under socialism) such as laundries, bakeries and so on meant that long hours had to be spent in food preparation and home care – tasks that were invariably seen as the responsibility of women.

Lane did concede that a socialist society such as the former USSR in the 1960s had made some significant advances in terms of men's and women's equality, for example in the collective ownership of the means of production. Nevertheless there remained powerful cultural forces and behaviour patterns that were a barrier to change towards equality between men and women in family life.

Mark G. Field carried out a survey of published material on the Soviet family, and he too found little evidence of the involvement of men in domestic and childcare tasks (Field 1968). Moreover, provision for very young children, crucial if women are to maintain continuity in their careers, was not as full or as widely available as necessary.

Hilda Scott, in a study of the formerly socialist Czechoslovakia, reached similar general conclusions concerning the changes that had occurred (Scott 1976). There were some improvements compared to the West, but cultural barriers and entrenched male patriarchal attitudes remained. She highlighted the inadequacy of state provision of childcare, which was not extensive enough to enable women to work alongside men on an equal basis.

An episode of the 1980s BBC TV documentary series *Lovelaw*, which examined marriage and family life around the world, featured a Hungarian married couple where the wife bemoaned how little work Hungarian men did in the house; her husband, she said, would not even lift a plate.

So such evidence as there is does not suggest that the establishment of a socialist society will automatically change women's lives in families for the better. This observation has led some feminists to attempt a more radical incorporation of feminist theory into their analysis. *Socialist feminists* maintain that women's oppression is rooted not only in capitalism but in an autonomous system of social organization that feminists term patriarchy. The relationship between these two systems is extremely complex, but it follows at once that overthrowing capitalism will not be enough: at the same time a struggle must be waged against the ideology and structures of patriarchy, central to which is the family.

Other feminists go further, and altogether reject socialist answers to gender inequality in society and within the family. Their views are the subject of the next chapter.

Bibliography and further reading

Barrett, M. and McIntosh, M. (1982) *The Anti-Social Family*, London: Verso

Benston, M. (1972) 'The political economy of women's liberation', in N. Glazer-Malbin and H.Y. Waehrer (eds) *Women in a Man-made World*, Chicago, Illinois: Rand McNally

Bernard, J. (1976) *The Future of Marriage*, Harmondsworth: Penguin

Coontz, S. and Henderson, P. (eds) (1986) *Women's Work, Men's Property*, London: Verso

Cooper, D. (1972) *The Death of the Family*, Harmondsworth: Penguin

Donzelot, J. (1980) *The Policing of Families*, London: Hutchinson

Engels, F. (1884) *The Origin of the Family, Private Property and the State*, 1985 edn, Harmondsworth: Penguin

Feeley, D. (1972) 'The family', in L. Jenness (ed.) *Feminism and Socialism*, New York: Pathfinder

Field, M.G. (1968) 'Workers (and mothers): Soviet women today', in D.R. Brown (ed.) *Women in the Soviet Union*, New York: Teachers College Press

Gough, K. (1972) 'An anthropologist looks at Engels', in N. Glazer-Malbin and H.Y. Waehrer (eds) *Woman in a Man-made World*, Chicago, Illinois: Rand McNally

Hartmann, H. (1981) 'The unhappy marriage of Marxism and feminism: towards a more progressive union', in L. Sargent (ed.) *Women and Revolution: A Discussion of the Unhappy Marriage of Marxism and Feminism*, London: Pluto Press

Lane, D. (1970) *Politics and Society in the USSR*, London: Weidenfeld & Nicolson

Lasch, C. (1977) *Haven in a Heartless World*, New York: Basic Books

Morgan, L.H. (1963) *Ancient Society: Researches in the Lines of Human Progress from Savagery through Barbarism to Civilization*, New York: Meridian

Scott, H. (1976) *Women and Socialism*, London: Allison & Busby

Zaretsky, E. (1976) *Capitalism, the Family and Personal Life*, London: Pluto Press

Essay questions

Evaluate the Marxist approach to the family.

Coursework suggestions

Conduct an investigation of one or more features of the Marxist approach through a small survey of families and households. For instance, you could seek evidence for the contention that the exploitation of women serves 'capitalist' interests.

5 Liberal and radical feminist approaches

Key ideas

- Patriarchy
- Liberal feminism
- Radical feminism
- Political and social changes affecting women
- Homosexual parenthood
- The domestic division of labour
- The symmetrical family
- The New Man
- Housework as ideology
- Decision making and power in households
- Money matters

Key figures

- Young and Wilmott
- Ann Oakley
- Jonathan Gershuny
- Melanie Henwood
- Ray Pahl
- Stephen Edgell

This chapter examines the work of feminists who do not subscribe to the Marxist or socialist-feminist approaches to the family.

Feminists who focus on patriarchy reject the notion that family life and gender relationships are reflections of the economic structure of society. They believe that the cultural and social aspects of male–female inequality are central to an understanding of the issues. It is not change at the economic level that is required to improve women's position within the family and society generally but changes in cultural and social behaviours that are based on patriarchy.

Theory	Source of oppression	Solution
Marxism (Engels)	Capitalism. Men's control of property. Women's lack of ownership of the means of production.	The overthrow of capitalism by political revolution. Under communism, the means of production will be communally owned, and childcare will be a communal responsibility. Men and women will work alongside each other and will be equal.
Marxist feminism	The economic exploitation of women in families. Women's lack of wealth and economic power.	
Feminist Marxism	The family as an ideological agent of exploitation. The socialization of children into capitalist values.	
Liberal feminism	Inequality of opportunity. Sexism embedded in the culture of society and the attitudes of individuals (particularly men).	Legislation for equal opportunity. The eradication of sexism from culture and attitudes. The socialization of children into a culture of equality.
Radical feminism	The tyranny of reproduction, the socialization of children into patriarchal values, and the threat and use of physical force. The family as a key instrument in maintaining male power.	Total independence of women from men (some radical feminists include reproductive independence). The abolition of the family.

Figure 5.1 Sources of women's oppression

Individually or in groups, think of some examples of 'cultural and social aspects of male–female inequality'.

The concept of patriarchy

Patriarchy is an all-embracing term which can be simply defined as male power and authority in society. One example is the common situation of the workplace where there are male bosses and female subordinates, as in the stereotype of the male manager and female secretary.

Wine bar

Very 'feminine' and 'nice' girl and slightly older man drinking after work in a wine bar.

Man Cheers

Girl Cheers *(drinks)*. Mmm, quite nice and fruity.

Man They know me here.

Girl Really? Because some white wines – they can sort of make you scrunch your bottom up, can't they? But this is quite cordial, isn't it?

Man Do you think you're going to enjoy working for the company?

Girl Oh, yes. It's a very choice powder-room, ever such unusual washbasins, quite opaque.

Man That's a very attractive dress, if I may say so.

Girl   Oh, do you like it? I think it makes me look a bit extinct, do you know what I mean? I like the fabric, though, it's quite commercialized.

Man   Do you have a boyfriend, or . . . ?

Girl   No, I don't really like steady relationships – they make me feel a bit Rice Krispie-ish, do you know what I mean?

Man   Because I'd really like to take you out one evening, if I may.

Girl   I don't think so.

Man   Because I'm married?

Girl   I don't really like going out with people from work – it all gets sort of conjugated.

Man   Nobody has to know.

Girl   It always does get out, though. Offices are really ostentatious for gossip, aren't they?

Man   Well, it wouldn't matter, would it?

Girl   Well, it's against company policy, isn't it? People going out with their secretaries. There might be a big sort of moussaka about it.

Man   Yes, but what could be the worst that could happen?

Girl   Well, the worst that could happen would be that Head Office found out and I had to fire you, Colin. Cheers.

Source: Victoria Wood, *Barmy*, London: Mandarin, 1987.

Think of a number of occupations where stereotypes are common. Imagine that the men and the women change roles, and make a note of the changes in behaviour patterns that you would expect to see. What would happen, for instance, if a man were secretary to a female boss?

If you are working in pairs or groups, you could work this activity into a role-play exercise.

Figure 5.2 A manifestation of patriarchy

If the idea or experience of female–male role reversal seems 'strange', you have become aware of how deeply entrenched such cultural attitudes are. Patriarchy finds expression in all areas of life. For instance, it is displayed as male dominance in institutions such as politics and the mass media.

Within the family, patriarchy is a feature of relations between husbands and wives, and fathers and children: the father/husband is dominant and powerful, whereas wives and children are comparatively powerless. Husbands expect wives to make their meals, do their washing and clean the house; fathers expect obedience from their children. All such interactions and behaviour patterns are manifestations of patriarchy.

In terms of what may be done to alter this situation, two broad positions can be identified: liberal feminism and radical (or pure) feminism (Bouchier 1983). Both approaches focus on patriarchy and see men as the 'problem' in many aspects of social life as well as in the family.

Liberal feminism

Liberal feminists can be described as offering a generally 'optimistic' view of the current position and prospects of women in society and in the family. Like functionalist sociologists (see Chapter 3) and advocates of the symmetrical family such as Young and Wilmott (discussed on page 67), they consider that progress has been made over time, so life in the present is an improvement on how things were in the past.

Liberal feminists see no need for a political or social revolution, as do other feminists; rather they see social change as evolutionary. They hold that in the latter part of the twentieth century we have witnessed significant improvements in relations between men and women and in family life. The direction of change has been towards egalitarianism (equality between the sexes).

The following are some of the changes that liberal feminists have identified as having improved the situation of women and families in our century:

Political and legal changes

- Votes for women were won in the early part of this century.

- Legislation mandating equal pay for men and women in the same jobs was enacted in the UK in the 1970s.

- Sexual discrimination has been made illegal, so that women are entitled to equal treatment in all walks of life as well as work, e.g. in access to financial loans and the terms of mortgages.

- Women enjoy property rights and inheritance on an equal basis to men.

- Rape in marriage was made a crime in the early 1990s.

- Domestic violence has recently become more clearly defined as a crime.

Social changes

- Men do more in the home than in the past. In the 1950s and 1960s their activities were confined mainly to home improvement and do-it-yourself, but more recently there has been a trend towards greater involvement in shared domestic labour (the symmetrical family).

- Men are more involved with childcare. There is greater emphasis on active fatherhood, and some men are spending more time at home with their families.

- Women are increasingly involved in formerly 'male' areas of life in leisure and sport.

- Men and women are more equal at work. Positive attempts have been made to get women into 'male' areas of work, for instance as engineers and scientists.

- Women in 1994 constituted over half the total workforce in Britain. Their earning power is a vital part of most families' income. If 'money is power', as W.H. Auden asserted, this could be seen as heralding very significant changes in power and social relationships.

- The majority of people in the West now enjoy better standards of living. They have access to labour-saving devices such as washing machines, dishwashers and vacuum cleaners that have made household tasks easier and less time consuming.

- Families are now smaller than they used to be, with fewer children, so more attention can be paid to the quality of family life. This can give women a chance to fulfil themselves in a variety of ways – through their careers and through sport and leisure activities – rather than devoting themselves entirely to their children and the family, their main option in the past.

How far do you agree that each of the above changes has been significant in improving women's lives? Make a note of points for and against.

Liberal feminists are not fully happy about the degree of change in all the above areas. But where things are still detrimental to wives and mothers, they believe that 'gentle' persuasion and 'consciousness raising' can convince men that change is for the benefit of all.

Do you agree that men can be 'persuaded' to change? Ideally you should discuss this topic in mixed-sex groups; otherwise make your own notes.

For liberal feminists 'revolutionary' change as favoured by Marxist feminists is both unnecessary and unfeasible. They see equality of the sexes as beneficial to both men and women: women have indeed gained from the social changes that have occurred, but men have also gained from their closer involvement with their children and family life. Children too have generally benefited from the better standard of living

Figure 5.3 Egalitarian family, shared childcare

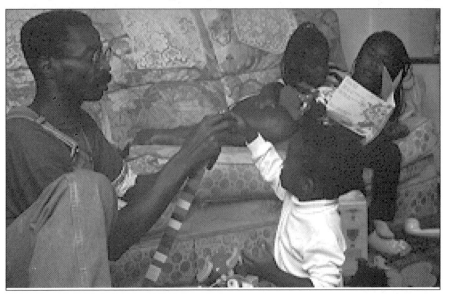

made possible when their mothers as well as their fathers earn an income, and children in smaller families gain from the increased attention and involvement of both parents.

 Look through a selection of magazines aimed at young women, and make note of any material that focuses on how to change men within marriage and families. What sorts of themes or strategies emerge? Do they echo a liberal feminist perspective? If so, in what ways?

Criticisms of liberal feminism

Liberal feminists certainly have popular support, and there is evidence that the changes outlined above have had effects on many women's lives. There is little sign in Western societies that the kinds of revolutionary political changes advocated by Marxist and socialist feminists will occur in the foreseeable future.

However, other feminists are often critical of liberal feminists for their somewhat cosy view, which perhaps reflects the experience of white, middle-class professional groups in occupations such as teaching, social work, the legal professions, the mass media and similar fields. (Of course a similar point may often be made about the backgrounds of more 'revolutionary' feminists too.)

Critics of liberal feminism point to a wealth of evidence from studies of the domestic division of labour (see pages 67–70) that husbands and fathers are still not greatly involved in housework and the more mundane aspects of childcare.

They cite studies highlighting the degree of domestic violence and marital rape to show that the more negative aspects of patriarchy are still much in evidence (see pages 79–81).

Wives main murder victims

Wives are the most frequent victims of family murders in the United States and 60 per cent of the assailants in spouse killings are husbands, according to a justice department study released yesterday.

The study reviewed more than 8,000 murder cases brought to court in 1988 in large urban counties and found that 16 per cent of them involved the killing of a family member.

It said 40 per cent of the family murders involved a spouse killing and a male was the assailant in two-thirds of the family murders. Among white couples involved in killings of spouses, the study found that wives were the victims in 62 per cent of the murders, but the number dropped to 53 per cent for blacks.

The study found children were killed by their parents at twice the rate that the children murdered their parents.

Alcohol usually was a factor in a family murder, with half of the killers drinking at the time of the killing.

Fourteen per cent of the family murderers had a history of mental illness.

Guardian, 11 July 1994

They point out that women's average earnings are still only around 70 per cent of men's. Despite the large proportion of female workers, the majority of women are concentrated in low-paid occupations and many work part time. These inequalities continue to have profound implications for family relationships.

1 What might be the relationship between a wife's level of earnings and the level of equality within a marriage? Explain your answer.

2 Conduct a small survey of your own family and relatives and those of other members of your sociology class to see if you can find a connection between earnings and the equality of husbands and wives.

It could be argued that wives who earn less and work shorter hours than their husbands are likely to do the greater proportion of housework and childcare. Some studies, such as *British Social Attitudes* (1992), suggest that part-time women workers who are married with children have the 'worst of all worlds' in that not only do they have a commitment to their work, but they are also expected to do the majority of domestic and childcare tasks.

Do you have female relatives who work part time? If so, does this observation apply to them?

Radical (or pure) feminism

Radical feminists reject both the idea that inequality and the oppression of women are caused by capitalism and the optimistic belief of the liberal feminists that changes for the better are gradually occurring. Radical feminists maintain that patriarchal power and authority are deeply embedded within the social structure of most societies whether these are capitalist or socialist, tribal or industrial.

There is a range of views within radical feminism. At one end of the spectrum there are 'softer' versions that see possibilities of change occurring within traditional family and household structures. Here there is a difference of degree from the 'gentle' persuasion of the liberal feminists: more active and militant approaches are required to pressurize men and society in general to accept equality between the sexes. The following are examples of radical-feminist campaigns:

- The Wages for Housework campaign in the 1980s advocated payment for housework by means of large increases in family allowances payable to women.

- Campaigns against domestic violence and marital rape have led to legislation and more sympathetic handling of such matters on the part of the police and legal authorities.

1 Conduct research in the library, using CD-ROM if available or newspapers, to find out as much as you can about the main feminist campaigns of the 1980s, and make detailed notes.

2 Can you find examples of similar campaigns in recent years?

So, compared to liberal feminists, 'softer' radical feminists engage in stronger and more direct action. They do not believe men will voluntarily surrender their patriarchal privileges. However, both liberal feminists and 'soft' radical feminists can be seen as reformist, since they believe that changes can occur within the existing institutions of work and family.

'Hard' or ultra-radical feminists are more pessimistic about the possibility of reforming the institutions that oppress women because they see such institutions as intrinsically oppressive. They believe the patriarchal monogamous family must be abolished, and alternative ways of living together must be encouraged. As well as being anti-family, some who subscribe to this approach are anti-men.

Get Your Facts Straight, Sister

The bestselling feminist writer, Susan Faludi, is 'irresponsible'; the *Beauty Myth* author, Naomi Wolf, a 'mad conspiracist'; and as for the doyenne of the women's movement, Gloria Steimen, she should 'get a life'.

Such swingeing criticisms of American feminists sound as though they might have come from one of that country's more intolerant male, right-wing commentators. In fact, they were uttered by a woman who is a feminist and distinguished academic. Big sisters, watch out – Christina Sommers is after you.

Sommer's book, *Who Stole Feminism: How Women Have Betrayed Women*, published this summer in America by Sinom & Schuster, has made this associate professor at Clark University, Masschusetts the most talked about feminist philosopher in American universities, and the hottest guest on television talk show.

Quite simply, Sommers claims that the statistical evidence on which some of the big names of radical feminism have founded their theories is, to say the least, misleading.

One target is Naomi Wolf, the author of *The Beauty Myth*, who reported that 150,000 women a year were dying of anorexia in America. It was a powerful argument in her theses that women are so subjugated by society that they can starve to death. The figure that Sommer's research turned up, however, and which is cited in her book, is fewer than 100. 'In fact', more people probably die from bee stings than anorexia, but of course, that would not convince people that men are monsters, and women are oppressed by them,' she says.

Sunday Times, 14 August 1994

Some feminists are lesbian and advocate lesbian couple relationships as the only route to true 'liberation' for women. Some lesbian couples raise children, and this has caused controversy, for instance when applications by lesbians to adopt children have attracted press attention. Probably the most common form of lesbian family, however, is where one of the partners is divorced and has custody of the children from a former heterosexual relationship. No clear figures are available, but the number of such households is probably quite small.

More controversial and a favourite subject of news headlines are cases where lesbian couples have children through artificial insemination or male sperm donors. The sperm donor is often a male homosexual friend of the couple who has little or no further involvement in the rearing of the child.

There has always been controversy on the subject of homosexual parenthood. Some see this as a way of life and choice that should be available as well as a way of counteracting patriarchal institutions such as the heterosexual nuclear family. Criticism has predictably been voiced by the New Right (see Chapter 8) and the conservative press, but homosexual couples and families have also attracted criticism from people of the same sexuality. Such critics say that homosexual couples and families are merely replicating the traditional nuclear family and do not really solve the problems and issues raised by that institution. For example, within a lesbian couple one partner might play a 'masculine' role and the other a 'feminine' role, in which case there would be little behavioural difference from a heterosexual couple.

Lesbians who seek to avoid reproducing the nuclear family look for an answer in communal living and group households, where there is a variety of relationships and childrearing patterns that are not based on the stereotypical nuclear family model.

Describe in detail what some of these 'alternative' living arrangements might be like.

What is the role of men in such a world? Some advocates of this view see little need for men to be involved in women's lives because whenever men are in relationships with women they seek to impose their patriarchal dominance to the detriment of the women. Male–female relationships, they believe, are the key source of women's oppression.

Explain this viewpoint, giving appropriate examples.

Critics of ultra-radical feminism see it as unrealistic and utopian in its anti-family and anti-male stance. A key problem is that large numbers of people, women and men, freely choose to live in conventional family structures. This matter of choice raises philosophical issues concerning whether people can exercise conscious free will or are subject to ideological pressures reinforced through social conditioning and socialization. Radical feminists would insist on the latter interpretation.

Discuss these two explanations of choice, making points for and against each of them. Take as your starting point this assertion: 'Most people are brought up to think that there is no alternative to living in families if one wishes to seek personal fulfilment and happiness in life.'

To illustrate some of the features of the theoretical issues we have been examining, we shall now consider two facets of family life:

* the domestic division of labour, and

* decision making in families.

The domestic division of labour

This term refers to how essential household tasks are shared out within families. The possibilities can be represented as shown in Table 5.1.

Table 5.1 The division of household responsibilities			
Household task	*Mainly men (%)*	*Mainly women (%)*	*Shared equally (%)*
Washing and ironing	2	88	9
Looking after sick children	2	67	30
Household cleaning	4	72	23
Preparing evening meals	6	77	17
Household shopping	7	50	43
Teaching children discipline	13	19	67
Doing evening dishes	22	39	36
Organizing household bills	32	38	30
Repairing household equipment	82	6	8

 Take each of the possibilities mentioned in the figure in turn, and explain how household tasks and childcare are divided out between husbands and wives (and possibly children).

The key question is, 'Who does what in the home?' A useful starting point is to consider the work of two British sociologists, Michael Young and Peter Wilmott. In their book *The Symmetrical Family* (1975), based on a study carried out in London, they refer to the way husbands' and wives' commitment and involvement in family life have evolved during this century towards a more egalitarian, symmetrical relationship. They see the family as having evolved through three stages:

1 The pre-industrial family. This family is a 'unit of production'; parents and children work as a team to provide food, clothing and shelter at a subsistence level.

2 The early industrial family. Here family members begin to go out to work and become 'wage earners'. Poverty and low wages could lead to the development of 'industrial extended families' as highlighted by Anderson (1980).

3 The symmetrical family. This developed in the twentieth century and became the home-centred nuclear family, distinct from the extended family. There are shared conjugal roles and a more egalitarian relationship between husbands and wives.

Features of the new family structure were the greater numbers of working wives and mothers and the greater involvement of husbands in household and domestic tasks. This can be seen as an early recognition of the 'New Man' who became a feature of mass media attention in the 1970s and 1980s.

Referring to Figure 5.4, what patterns of change occurred between 1974 and 1987? Explain the changes and describe their impact on family life.
   Table 5.1 shows the results of a survey about how married couples in Britain shared various responsibilities. Do these results provide evidence of an egalitarian, symmetrical relationship?

A family that is described as symmetrical is not necessarily one for which tasks in the home have become 'gender neutral', i.e. no longer thought of as being tasks generally carried out by either women or men. It has become difficult to predict 'who does

Figure 5.4 Changes in the work patterns of married couples between 1974/5 and 1987

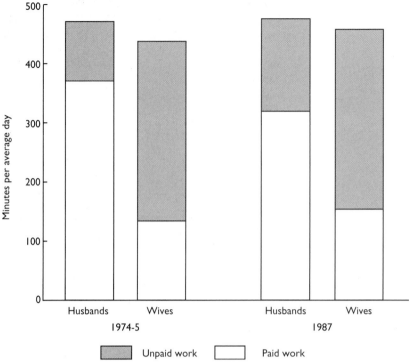

Source: Gershuny, 1992, p. 78

what' in any one house. Symmetry as defined refers more to balance: the proportion of *time* spent on household and childcare activities is roughly equal between men and women. Husbands may still carry out stereotypical 'male' tasks, such as:

- car maintenance,

- decorating, and

- repairs and technical activities,

and wives continue to perform stereotypical 'female' tasks, such as:

- cleaning,

- washing, and

- ironing.

These tasks are done on the basis of an equal commitment or outlay of time by both marital partners.

As stated previously, there are similarities between the views on gradual change for the better put forward by liberal feminists and the empirical work of Young and Wilmott.

In contrast, Ann Oakley's book *The Sociology of Housework* (1974a), published at about the same time as *The Symmetrical Family*, provided a very different picture of the division of labour in British households at that time. Theoretically, Oakley's approach is associated with a radical-feminist position, and for many years she has been regarded as Britain's foremost feminist sociologist. She carried out detailed qualitative interview research among housewives in London and found that in the majority of cases most housework was carried out by women and that men played little part in domestic tasks.

Several interesting issues arise from Oakley's work, such as the way housework is seen by women as boring, monotonous and full of drudgery. This is an image far removed from that portrayed in women's magazines and advertising, where housework and homemaking are presented as fulfilling and creative.

Another key finding in Oakley's work concerns the aspects of gender identity associated with housework as typified in the following quotes from respondents:

'I don't agree with men doing housework. I don't think it's a man's job . . . I certainly wouldn't like to see my husband cleaning a room up.'

'I don't think it's mannish for a man to stay at home. I like a man to be a man.'

 These two statements were made more than twenty years ago. Do you think that many women today would still agree with the views expressed? Give reasons for your answer, incorporating consideration of social class and ethnicity in your explanation.

Ideas about femininity associated with housework can be interpreted from either or both of two perspectives:

* From an *ideological* perspective, women's beliefs and ideas about housework and femininity are seen to reflect society's dominant beliefs and ideas as conveyed through agencies such as schools and the mass media.

* An emphasis on *gender socialization* focuses on the way boys and girls are socialized within families into appropriate male and female behaviour patterns that reflect adult roles and an essentially stereotypical division of household responsibilities.

1 Research magazines and similar sources to find examples of the link between femininity and housework.

2 Think of examples of how gender socialization works, using personal examples where appropriate.

Young and Wilmott clearly differ from Oakley in their conclusions about the changing nature of housework and home-related activities. The best way to evaluate this disagreement is to consider the evidence from more recent research. A cursory examination of the relevant studies shows considerable support for Oakley's conclusions. Family studies carried out by Ray Pahl (1984) and Melanie Henwood (1987), the latest *British Social Attitudes* report and more recent interpretive studies (see Chapter 7) show that most housework and childcare are still done by women. Even in recent studies, this remains true when wives and mothers go out to work on a full-time or part-time basis.

Conduct a brief survey, either in class or in your neighbourhood, to test this hypothesis: 'Women in the 1990s are still responsible for the majority of housework and domestic activities.'

A major study by Jonathan Gershuny (1992) of changes in the domestic division of labour in the UK from 1975 to 1987 lends some support to Young and Wilmott's thesis of the symmetrical family. Gershuny used time-budget analysis of detailed diaries kept by respondents on a day-to-day and weekly basis. He also examined cross-cultural evidence from European and Canadian studies. He found a clear trend towards men carrying out the more routine domestic activities in greater proportions than formerly, particularly when wives go out to work, so in this sense there is support for the idea of the symmetrical family. However, when women go out to work their total working hours, including domestic activities, still remain greater than men's, which undermines the notion that there has been a significant shift towards equality between men and women.

Gershuny concludes on an optimistic note by saying that there is evidence of 'a really very substantial social change over the last couple of decades – and [trends] provide the basis for a not unhopeful view of the future of the household.' Young and Wilmott also saw the symmetrical family as a trend, and many sociologists would agree that some changes have occurred in the way domestic and childcare tasks are arranged between husbands and wives. The move towards a more privatized, home-centred family has been a part of this.

In summary, then, two positions have emerged concerning the degree of change in the domestic division of labour:

- There is a significant trend towards a more egalitarian future in marriages and households. This is the 'symmetrical family' and liberal-feminist position.

- The changes that have occurred have been relatively insignificant and have made little impact on the unequal burden of domestic labour and childcare borne by women. This is the position adopted by Ann Oakley and the radical feminists.

Decision making and power in households

As well as the domestic division of labour, issues of power and authority in families are part of the feminists' detailed examination of patriarchy. One focus has been on the way decisions are made about aspects of home and family life.

An early study of these issues was carried out by Stephen Edgell (1980). Edgell examined decision making in middle-class families to see if there was a trend towards more democratic and egalitarian relationships. His choice of a middle-class sample was based on the view that the behaviour patterns of the middle classes are a predictor of eventual trends in the wider society.

List and explain some behaviour that originated with the middle classes and spread through the wider society. (One example is drinking wine in Britain.)

Edgell's findings tend to call into question the idea of symmetricality, as can be seen from Table 5.3.

Jan Pahl (1989) examines a specific issue concerning gender differences in power and decision making between husbands and wives – the control of money. Responses to the question 'Who really controls the money that comes into this house?' revealed a complex pattern of control that could be summarized in four possibilities:

Table 5.2 The importance, frequency and pattern of decision making in different areas of family life

Decision area (majority pattern)\{/D\}	Perceived importance	Frequency	Decision maker
Moving	Very important	Infrequent	Husband
Finance	Very important	Infrequent	Husband
Car	Important	Infrequent	Husband
House	Very important	Infrequent	Husband and wife
Children's education	Very important	Infrequent	Husband and wife
Holidays	Important	Infrequent	Husband and wife
Weekends	Not important	Frequent	Husband and wife
Other leisure activities	Not important	Frequent	Husband and wife
Furniture	Not important	Infrequent	Husband and wife
Interior decorations	Not important	Frequent	Wife
Food and other domestic spending	Not important	Frequent	Wife
Children's clothes	Not important	Frequent	Wife

Source: Stephen Edgell, *Middle Class Couples*, London: George Allen & Unwin, 1980

- *Wife control*, where there is no joint bank account and the wife pays the bills. This was common in low-income working-class households.

- *Wife-controlled pooling*, where there is a joint bank account and the wife sorts out the main bills and supervises expenditure. This occurred in middle-income households, where there was a likelihood of both partners working. The more the wife earned relative to her husband, the more likely she was to be in control of finances.

- *Husband-controlled pooling*, where there is a joint bank account and the husband is in control, paying bills and checking expenditure. This was found in higher-income groups where the wife was probably in a lower-paid or part-time job.

- *Husband control*, where there is no joint bank account, the husband has his own account, sorts out expenditure and gives his wife housekeeping money. If a wife worked, her earnings typically went towards the housekeeping.

Discuss in pairs or make notes on the following questions:

1 *Which of the four types of control over money gives (a) wives and (b) husbands more power?*

2 *Which is the most patriarchal?*

3 *Which arrangement would correspond with a symmetrical family?*

4 *With relation to current trends in employment patterns, which of the four will probably become most common?*

Table 5.3 Marital happiness by control of finances: wives' answers (husbands' in brackets)

	Wife control	Wife-controlled pooling	Husband-controlled pooling	Husband control
Marriage described as:				
Happy/very happy	13(13)	23(25)	37(35)	13(16)
Average/unhappy	1(1)	4(2)	2(4)	9(6)
Total number of couples	14	27	39	22

Source: Janice Pahl, *Money and Marriage*, London: Macmillan, 1989

5 Which of the four types do you think results in the happiest relationships, and why?

Now compare your answer with findings summarized in Table 5.3 on page 71 (Pahl 1993).

1 Which marriages are the most happy? Which the least? Try to explain why.

2 Are any of the findings surprising for a feminist? If so, why?

3 What needs to be done in terms of control over money to make marriages happier?

4 Is there a methodological problem with measuring 'happiness'? Explain what it might be.

A clear-cut picture of straightforward patriarchy does not emerge from Jan Pahl's work, but there is some evidence to support feminist arguments about male control and power in a significant proportion of marriages.

Conclusion

This chapter, like the previous one, has focused on some of the most important debates and issues concerning our understanding of families and households in contemporary societies. Feminist perspectives have been significant in enhancing our understanding of vital areas of gender inequality and male–female relationships both in families and in the wider society. The debate continues; the answers that are offered range from those that are optimistic and see continuing improvement in the position of women within conventional family structures to those that do not see this occurring and advocate radical and sweeping changes in the way people live and conduct their relationships.

Bibliography and further reading

Anderson, M. (ed.) (1980) *Sociology of the Family*, Harmondsworth: Penguin

Bouchier, D. (1983) *The Feminist Challenge*, London: Macmillan

Edgell, S. (1980) *Middle-Class Couples*, London: Allen & Unwin

Gershuny, J. (1992) 'Change in the domestic division of labour in the UK, 1975–1987', in N. Abercrombie and A. Warde (eds) *Social Change in Contemporary Britain*, Cambridge: Polity Press

Henwood, M. (1987) *Inside the Family*, London: Family Policy Studies Centre

Jowell, R., Brook, L., Prior, G. and Taylor, B. (eds) (1992) *British Social Attitudes: The 9th Report*, Aldershot: SCPR Dartmouth Publishing

Oakley, A. (1974a) *The Sociology of Housework*, Oxford: Martin Robertson

—— (1974b) *Housewife*, London: Allen Lane

Pahl, J. (1989) *Money and Marriage*, London: Macmillan

—— (1993) 'Money, marriage and ideology: holding the purse strings?', *Sociology Review*, vol. 3, no. 1

Pahl, R. (1984) *Divisions of Labour*, Oxford: Blackwell

Young, M. and Wilmott, P. (1975) *The Symmetrical Family*, Harmondsworth: Penguin

Essay questions

1 Examine the view that marriage and family life have become equal partnerships.

2 'The "New Man" is as mythical a creature as "the Abominable Snowman".' Discuss.

Coursework suggestions

Devise and conduct a study similar to Jan Pahl's (pages 70–2), using your family and relatives and friends who are married to see if control over money is a factor in determining whether relationships are egalitarian, matriarchal or patriarchal.

Stimulus – response questions

Item A

Final say by employment status of couple

	Both Unemployed	Man employed woman unemployed	Man unemployed, woman full-time	Man unemployed, woman part-time	Both employed, full-time	Man employed, woman part-time	Other
Husband	(35) 16.5%	(44) 26.7%	(2) 7.1%	(7) 15.9%	(17) 11.0%	(28) 16.1%	(1) 8.3%
Wife	(76) 35.8%	(28) 17.0%	(3) 10.7%	(20) 45.5%	(35) 22.7%	(34) 19.5%	
Joint	(61) 28.8%	(61) 37.0%	(14) 50.0%	(12) 27.3%	(74) 48.1%	(66) 37.9%	(10) 83.3%
Disagree	(40) 18.9%	(32) 19.4%	(9) 32.1%	(5) 11.4%	(28) 18.2%	(45) 25.9%	(1) 8.3%

Source: L. Morris (1993) Household Finance management and the labour market: a case study in Hartlepool, Sociological Review, Vol 41 No 3, pp 506–536

'Final say' refers to which partner has the final say over spending. Both partners were asked questions on this. The table indicates, in the 'disagree' row, the cases where couples disagreed on who had the final say.

Women's influence within the home would then appear to be greatest in cases which require close monitoring of low income, principally where the man is unemployed. Women's position is also enhanced, albeit to a lesser extent, in cases of dual employment, though here joint authority is the majority outcome. These results are also reflected in the finding that women's final say falls as household income rises, with joint final say, and to a lesser extent men's final say, rising with income.

Source: L. Morris (1993) 'Household financial management and the labour market: a case study in Hartlepool', *Sociological Review*, Vol. 41, No. 3, pp. 506–36.

Item B

'The family is the place where we care for each other, where we practise consideration for each other. Caring families are the basis of a society that cares.' Prime Minister James Callaghan (Labour), 1978.

This much quoted statement about the nature of family life comes from a speech made by James Callaghan when he was Prime Minister in 1978. Taken out of context it is quite plain. He was doing as politicians of various persuasions have done for many years: justifying government policies which were restricting access to state provision of services, by extolling the superior virtues of family support. The use of the word 'caring' gives the hint that women are seen as the most suitable providers of such assistance. It is as much prescription as description. There is a long history in Britain of politicians describing family life as they would like it to be, but presenting that description as if it were a simple account of how most people live in reality. The implication is clear of course: if we don't live like this, then we ought to.

Source: Janet Finch (1989) *Family Obligations and Social Change*, Polity Press, p. 237.

Item C

As many have commented through the centuries, young males are essentially barbarians for whom marriage – meaning not just the wedding vows, but the act of taking responsibility for a wife and children – is an indispensable civilizing force. Supporting a family is a central means for a man to prove that he is a 'mensch'. Young men who don't work don't make good marriage material.

'Mensch' = a 'real man'

Source: Adapted from Charles Murray (1990) *Underclass*, 'The Emerging British Underclass', IEA.

(a) With reference to the table in Item A:
    (i) When are wives most likely to have the 'final say'? **(1 mark)**

(ii) When are husbands most likely to have the 'final say' **(1 mark)**

(b) With reference to Item A and elsewhere, what patterns have sociologists identified in terms of conjugal roles in families in Britain? **(8 marks)**

(c) How has social policy affected family structure and women's role in it? (Item B) **(6 marks)**

(d) What sociological perspective do the views expressed in Item C most closely resemble? **(1 mark)**

(e) Evaluate different sociological explanations for women's position in the labour market (Items B and C). **(8 marks)**

6 Radical psychiatry and other critical approaches

> **Key ideas**
>
> - The family as an emotionally repressive institution
> - Mental illness and the family
> - The dark side of family life
> - Domestic violence
> - Surveillance and control of family and private life
>
> **Key figures**
>
> - R.D. Laing
> - David Cooper
> - Michel Foucault
> - Dobash and Dobash
> - Jan Pahl
> - Dennis Marsden
> - M. Faulk
> - Erin Pizzey

This chapter continues our examination of approaches that are in some way or another critical of the contemporary family. The main theories covered so far have been structuralist in emphasis: in essence they look at families and households within the context of the wider social structure. This 'macro' emphasis has not been the only approach within sociology, however. Some sociologists following in the tradition of action sociology, rooted in the work of Max Weber (1864–1920) and Alfred Schutz (1899–1959), have developed a more micro approach, now referred to as interpretive sociology.

Structural sociologists of the family do not deal directly with the daily lives of families and their members. They concentrate on macro-level themes such as the role of the family in society, which they may characterize as:

- industrial, as in the functionalist approach;

- capitalist, as Marxists and socialist feminists would define it; or

- patriarchal, which is the key term for radical feminists.

Interpretive sociologists concentrate their attention on the details of people's lives in their everyday worlds of families and households. In some senses Ann Oakley's work, which we examined in the last chapter, adopted a micro approach, particularly in her use of detailed qualitative interviews to get a close picture of the lives of housewives.

Figure 6.1 The two sociologies

	Structuralist	**Interpretist**
Focus	Macro - large-scale study	Micro - small-scale study
Unit of analysis	Society	Interaction
Research	Social surveys, quantitative techniques	Qualitative, observational, in-depth techniques
Key theme	The role of the family in society in relation to other social instructions	What occurs in families and how family life, roles and responsibilities are negotiated and understood.

As with structuralist approaches, the term interpretive sociology embraces a diverse range of traditions, some of which we will meet in this chapter and the next.

Radical psychiatry and the dark side of family life

Some of the main contributors to the radical psychiatry approach, particularly R.D. Laing and David Cooper, were originally trained and worked as psychiatrists. However, they became increasingly critical of this field of work, with its assumptions about mental illness and its use of 'treatments' such as drugs, electro-convulsive therapy and incarceration.

In the 1960s, Laing and Cooper developed a more sociological approach which came to be known as anti-psychiatry. They rejected traditional psychiatry's focus on individual mentally ill patients who were deemed to be 'sick' and in need of medical treatment, and insisted that the group and wider social circumstances of the mentally ill needed to be taken into account. They started to see the family, and in particular the close-knit, privatized, inward-looking nuclear family of modern societies, as implicated in the production of mental illness in individuals.

They focused on one particular form of mental illness, schizophrenia, which is commonly associated with dual or alternative identities. The anti-psychiatrists correctly pointed out that schizophrenia was not a precise medical term with a prescribed list of symptoms, but was a blanket term used to cover a range of behaviour disorders that varied widely. They concentrated on the more interpretive sociological aspects of mental illness and deviance associated with stereotyping and labelling theory. In their view, people who do not conform to the accepted norms, values and behaviour patterns of the wider society are stigmatized, categorized as deviant and treated accordingly. They become 'cases' to be dealt with by professional 'experts' such as doctors, counsellors and psychiatrists.

In their book *Sanity, Madness and the Family* (1970) Laing and Esterson featured several case studies of families in which someone had been diagnosed as suffering from schizophrenia. This person was commonly the only child in a family, usually a daughter. In a typical case, some time after puberty the patient had become increasingly withdrawn, and after being sent to her family doctor she was referred to a psychiatrist, who diagnosed schizophrenia. Laing was interested in why this type of family setting should provide such a significant proportion of cases. Using Freudian theories from his psychoanalytic professional background, he deduced a complex pattern of family dynamics that were riddled with anxieties, tensions and conflicts.

The daughter was approaching sexual maturity and could be seen as a younger version of her mother by her father. Elements of jealousy fed by unconscious incestuous desires led to family rows over the daughter's staying out late and meeting boyfriends, with the suspicion that sexual relationships might be developing. Her mother was reaching the end of her 'reproductive' life cycle and was concerned about the loss of physical attractiveness associated with ageing, and her anxieties were also off-loaded on the confused daughter. Finally the daughter 'withdrew' from this world of rows and emotional tensions, refusing to communicate and behaving in a 'strange' manner that involved assuming other identities. This was interpreted as some sort of nervous breakdown, and eventually schizophrenia was diagnosed.

Laing suggested that this type of family situation was 'schizophrenogenic' (schizophrenia producing) and that the whole family needed to undergo therapy. In line with this analysis there grew up a school of family therapy, which is now an important approach to dealing with a range of behavioural disorders. Laing himself was closely associated with a family therapy centre where intense and detailed analysis of family interactions was carried out by experts with a view to correcting a psychologically damaging pattern of behaviour.

 Comment critically on this analysis, perhaps considering how easy or otherwise it might be to test its validity. Discuss the issues in pairs if you are working in a class context.

As with Freud's theories, Laing's analysis can be seen as plausible but controversial because it is based on reasonings and conjectures that are difficult to validate scientifically. Moreover there are other possible explanations of the root cause of tensions in families with adolescent daughters, which could be to do with less controversial issues such as parental concern about the personal safety of the daughter out on the streets. However, mental illness would not be an expected outcome in such circumstances.

 Discuss in pairs or make notes on why daughters rather than sons are the focus of such concerns. What differences might there be in families with a male adolescent?

Laing's critical views were echoed by David Cooper (1972), who saw the family as an ideological conditioning device that crushes the self and individual identity, subsuming them into the family. Cooper advocated that we break free from these 'chains' to produce more creative and independent individuals.

 Is it possible to bring children up in ways that would produce the 'free' individuals favoured by Cooper? How would this be done? These questions can be discussed in class or undertaken as an individual exercise.

Criticisms of the radical psychiatrists

Laing and the other radical psychiatrists certainly paint a picture of family life very different from the stable and harmonious institution portrayed by the functionalists. Some critics have said that Laing has presented a far too gloomy and negative portrait based on a small number of clinical cases of extreme family situations where mental illness was involved. The argument concerns how closely such cases reflect the position in the majority of families. Laing maintained that the lives of the family members in his clinical studies revealed the reality behind the façade of many 'normal' families.

Draw up a list of families portrayed in 'sitcoms' and soap operas such as Roseanne. How closely do they correspond to the 'Langian' model, and in what ways?

David Morgan (1975) identifies three kinds of problem with Laing's approach to the family:

- Laing presents an unbalanced portrait, focusing on the suffocating aspects of family life, whereas family life can also feature harmonious aspects and positive values encapsulated in the notion of the 'brotherhood of man'. In common parlance the word 'family' is often used to describe closeness and affection even between people who are not related. The terms 'sister' and 'brother' have long been used as expressions of comradeship and solidarity between unrelated people, for example within feminist, socialist, trade union and religious organizations.

- Laing focuses almost exclusively on parent–child interaction as the key to understanding the family. Parents, according to Laing, are powerful agents of socialization and children are powerless, and these dynamics are comparatively unaffected by outside forces. Morgan points out that children themselves can exert power in their interaction with parents, who may give in to their demands – as with the 'spoilt child'. Moreover siblings can have different effects on each other and on their parents. Children and families are in fact affected by external agencies and people – at work, at school, in peer groups, and in their exposure to the mass media and welfare workers.

Wheedling: study finds minors are masters of manipulation

Parents have always known it but now scientists have proved it – children are brilliant psychological manipulators in getting their own way.

Children as young as seven employ sophisticated negotiation strategies to wheedle gifts out of their parents.

'Bribery, negotiations and coercion were seen as being part of daily life by both parents and children irrespective of socio-economic background,' said Professor Herbert Walker.

Guardian, 9 September 1994

- Similarly Laing treats the family as if it were devoid of a social context. On the one hand the Laingian family seems to exist in a social vacuum, yet on the other it is universalized. No attention is paid to how childrearing practices are defined in a culture, to the links between the family and other social institutions, or to the options available to family members. Social class and related social structural characteristics that affect family life are not taken into account.

1 *'We're just like one big happy family here.' Who might be saying this, and to whom?*

2 *Examine class and ethnic differences in family life and show how they can affect interactions between family members, such as husbands and wives or parents and children.*

Feminist critics have pointed to the radical psychiatrists' 'gender-neutral' assumptions in their treatment of power and parent–child interactions, so issues of patriarchy and the oppression of women in families are not dealt with specifically. Defenders of Laing say that he did go some way along that road but such issues were not his prime focus.

Morgan also charges that Laing gives little indication of how we may escape the dilemmas he describes. There is no reassurance that alternative ways of ordering sexual and intimate relationships and parenting could lead to a more satisfactory state of affairs. After all, children have to be raised and brought up in some sort of interaction with adults.

How do you think children could be brought up to encourage them to become 'free', 'independent', 'creative' human beings?

Attempts at creating 'alternative family' environments for bringing up children are examined in Chapter 11.

As a final comment it is worth noting that in an interview shortly before his death Laing spoke in somewhat positive ways about his own life and family experiences, suggesting that he could not have envisaged a more desirable context in which to live.

Domestic violence

The radical psychiatrists have highlighted the emotional tensions that family life can involve, and feminists have highlighted male power in marriages. These approaches combine when the issues of domestic violence and abuse are considered.

A clear picture emerges from studies and more general accounts in the mass media that men, whether as husbands or as fathers, are responsible for the great majority of violence against other family members. Female violence is rare, although in some cases, particularly a wife's violence to a husband, it may be under-recorded.

Make brief notes or hold a group discussion to explain why the incidence of women's attacks on men might be under-recorded.

A number of studies since the 1970s (Dobash and Dobash 1979, Pahl 1985, Marsden 1976, Faulk 1980) have shown how widespread family violence is. It is not restricted

Women seek halt to male violence

More than 70 per cent of boys believe they are likely to use violence against women in future relationships and more than 60 per cent of men say they would respond violently to their partner in certain situations.

The statistics were highlighted yesterday at the launch of Zero Tolerance, a campaign that aims to challenge the acceptance of violence against women. One of the campaign's posters reads: 'He gave her flowers, chocolates and multiple bruising.'

Nearly 50 per cent of all murders of women are by a present or former partner and 40 per cent of homeless women are in that situation because of abuse.

Domestic violence account for 25 per cent of all reported crimes, according to Victim Support, and a police survey found that 70 per cent of women said the crime that worried them most was rape.

The Times, 19 January 1994

to the stereotypical drunken labourer on a Saturday night but exists among all socio-economic classes and income groups. Some of these studies show the appalling levels of injury that are inflicted, and note that they are often not reported.

Explain why you think female victims of serious domestic violence may not report these attacks.

In recent years there has been some evidence that the authorities – the police and the courts – have begun to pay more serious attention to family violence than they once did. Some regional police forces now have domestic violence units headed by senior officers (often women). Rape in marriage was classed as a crime in the early 1990s. Media attention to marital violence has perhaps helped to expose it as unacceptable, following on from the pioneering work of women's groups and organizations such as the Women's Refuge Movement in the 1970s.

Radical feminists remain unconvinced, however, that the problem is being satisfactorily addressed. They see male violence against women as symptomatic of the patriarchal power relations that dominate family life, and they believe that men still resort to violence to impose their will in very many families.

A problem with determining whether such violence is increasing or decreasing concerns the increased awareness through the media of crimes of family violence, resulting in larger numbers of convictions. This is not to say that things were any better in the past. As Erin Pizzey, the founder of the Women's Refuge Movement, put it in the title of her best-selling book, in former times it was often advisable for a woman to *Scream Quietly or the Neighbours Will Hear*.

 1 Hold a class discussion on the question, 'Is family violence decreasing?' Make a list of points for and against the case that it is.

*2 Using historical sources from the library, examine whether there was a
'Golden Age' when there was little family violence.*

Another equally distressing aspect of family violence is the abuse of children. Again, the perpetrators are overwhelmingly men, though in this case more of the assaults are carried out by stepfathers than by natural fathers. We will be examining step-parenting further in Chapter 10, pages 151–4.

Michel Foucault's critical approach to the family

Some important aspects of Foucault's work were introduced in Chapter 4 in the context of Marxist analyses of the family. His work also follows on from some of the issues raised by the anti-psychiatrists, particularly in the field of the 'micro' aspects of power in society. This focus differs from the structuralist aspect of Marxism, which sees the state as central to understanding the nature of power and how this relates to family structure.

In fact, Foucault saw 'power' differently from both the radical psychiatrists and the Marxists. For him, power is diffused throughout society as a characteristic of social relationships, including the family, but can also be found in the knowledge base of society as exercised by 'thought police' such as teachers, doctors, psychiatrists and social workers. These issues were raised in Chapter 4 in the context of Marxism as an alternative to 'liberal democratic' views that see such agencies as supporting the family when needed, but in the main leaving the family to its own private concerns. Foucault disagreed, maintaining like the Marxists that the wider society is heavily involved in modern family life. There is routine state intervention to control domestic life and family relations via the operation of the law, social work, the social security and tax and welfare systems.

Give examples of how the family has been affected by these 'state agencies'.

Foucault referred to these interventions as 'regulations through the family'. Society supports a particular kind of family life that is based on a monogamous nuclear family with a breadwinner husband, dependent wife and children. Any deviation from this stereotypical norm can be corrected by laws (for example, bigamy is illegal in Britain), social workers (who can remove children from families) and other similar 'corrective' agencies.

One theme in Foucault's work is the way conventional ideas of motherhood are reinforced. Mothers of young children who wish to work face difficulties in arranging satisfactory childcare, so their opportunities are restricted compared to men's. In Foucault's terms the 'message' that is being conveyed to such mothers is that going out to work is not 'normal'. Many such women experience guilt and stress which can be indirectly related to the 'social disapproval' they encounter.

Another feature of Foucault's work that is relevant to family life concerns historical change in the nature of sexuality, which has increasingly become a focus for attention and intervention in modern societies. There is an emphasis on 'discipline', meaning the ability to conform to a norm of performance and behaviour, and 'confession' – which in the modern world means confessing to lay experts (counsellors, doctors, psychiatrists) about one's 'inadequacies', such as premature ejaculation. The comedian

Victoria Wood captured the sense of inadequacy and anxiety that Foucault was highlighting: 'I'm not very good at sex. I filled in one of those questionnaires. They sent it back marked VERY POOR WORK.'

Foucault also noted historical changes in the controls that society exercises over the formation of families. In the past the main concern (especially of the upper classes) was with marriage alliances between lineages, but in recent times there has been a shift towards two forms of 'power over life' which have had implications for contemporary families:

- Social control of the body's biological and psychological life forces (for example, through stress on reproduction within monogamous marriage, condemnation of homosexuality as a 'perversion', etc.). Here the focus is upon integrating individuals efficiently into the economic, political and social systems in which they are called upon to play their part.

- A focus on the demographic characteristics of national populations, upon which the strength of nation states depends. Issues here include birth rates, life expectancy and levels of physical and mental well-being.

Morgan (1985) summarizes Foucault's main theses on sexuality as follows:

- The greater openness about sex seemingly in evidence today is a superficial liberation. While controls are more diffuse and apparently non-repressive, a sexual yardstick has been established against which one is expected to measure one's own performance, and there is now an obligation to work at and enjoy sex.

- The learning of sexual techniques requires teachers, counsellors, sexologists and related 'experts' as well as a whole sex industry of manuals, videos, magazines, books and literature within a network of clinics and therapy centres.

- There is an overlap between sex, truth and confession. Confession to 'experts' (doctors, therapists) about 'problems' (sexual dysfunction) parallels the idea of religious confession as the path to truth.

- There is an 'artificial unity' of 'sex' linking a diversity of concerns, practices and theories. The emotional, the biological, the interpersonal and the moral are merged so that 'sex' becomes a taken-for-granted 'fact of life' tied into marriage and the family. Morgan sees this trend as important in the development of individualization and the depoliticization of people's lives.

Take any of the above aspects of Foucault's work and explain how it offers a different perspective to the conventional one about issues of sexuality in a modern society.

The following example may help to illustrate Foucault's approach to sexuality. Imagine a man who consults his doctor for help because he is suffering from impotence. He tells of pressure at work arising from his employer's demands for higher productivity. This has caused sleeplessness, stress and sexual dysfunction. The doctor refers the man to a psychosexual counsellor, who gives advice on techniques to correct the problem. Drugs may be prescribed and, if the problem persists, further 'treatment' and therapy will be recommended.

Foucault and other critical theorists would point out that the root cause, i.e. the nature of the man's work in a pressurized and competitive society, is not dealt with. Marxists would see the nature of such work as endemic in a capitalist society and advocate revolution and the establishment of a socialist society. Foucault was pessimistic about the possibility of the Marxist 'solution'.

> *Which of the two approaches to the man's problem – one focusing on the individual's responsibility and the other society's – provides a more satisfactory answer?*

Foucault's work offers an approach that is distinctively different from those of both mainstream sociology and the anti-psychiatrists. He treated concepts such as power and social control in new and thought-provoking ways that add to the critical perspective on developments in the modern family. He opened the most personal aspects of our lives, including family life, to scrutiny within a sociological context. His was a gloomy view: he offered no clear solutions, unlike the Marxists and feminists. As with other French philosophical writers, Foucault's work is also difficult to read. Nevertheless, there is much of interest in his wide-ranging and demanding approach.

Conclusion

This chapter has examined work coming from traditions that are diverse but united in their critical approach to the family. The anti-psychiatrists focus on the psychodynamic aspects on family life, while Foucault points to the origins of the family's destructive tendencies in the wider social sphere.

This chapter completes the section that started with Chapter 4 and that has considered a variety of critical approaches to the family. The next two chapters complete the theory part of the book: Chapter 7 will examine phenomenological approaches, which are in the interpretive sociological tradition, and Chapter 8 will look at the contribution of the New Right to current debates about the family.

Figure 6.2 Critical approaches to the oppressive nature of the family

Critical approaches	Cause of the oppressive nature of the family
Marxist feminism	Capitalist values are reflected in family structures, which provide the means for the oppressed male worker to relieve his tensions by oppressing his wife and children.
Radical feminism	Patriarchy is a feature of relations between husbands and wives and between fathers and children. The family is a key instrument in maintaining male power.
Radical psychiatry	The family is riddled with tensions, anxieties and conflicts. It is an ideological conditioning device that crushes and absorbs individual identity.
Foucault	The norms of behaviour required by the state have become internalized by families and households. The power and authority to enforce these norms are wielded by state agencies and individual freedom is curtailed.

Bibliography and further reading

Cooper, D. (1972) *The Death of the Family*, Harmondsworth: Penguin

Dobash, R. and Dobash, R. (1979) *Violence Against Wives*, Wells: Open Books

Faulk, M. (1980) 'Men who assault women', in M. Strauss, R.J. Gelles and S. Steinmetz (eds) *Behind Closed Doors: Violence in the American Family*, New York: Doubleday

Laing, R.D. and Esterson, A. (1970) *Sanity, Madness and the Family*, Harmondsworth: Penguin

Marsden, D. (1978) 'Sociological perspectives on family violence', in J. Martin (ed.) *Violence and the Family*, Chichester: John Wiley

Morgan, D.H.J. (1975) *Social Theory and the Family*, London: Routledge & Kegan Paul

— (1985) *The Family, Politics and Social Theory*, London: Routledge

Pahl, J. (1985) *Marital Violence and Public Policy*, London: Routledge

Smith, B. (1985) *Michel Foucault*, Chichester: Ellis Horwood/Tavistock

Essay questions

'Yes, there is such a thing as spouse abuse, but, defined in any serious way, it is statistically uncommon' – Charles Murray. Discuss.

Coursework suggestions

Conduct an investigation into whether family violence is now treated differently by the authorities (police, courts, social services) than in the past. Is there a police domestic violence unit in your area? If so, could you arrange an interview? How do social workers and social services departments deal with such matters? Contact local women's organizations, such as Well Women Clinics, to find out about their involvement.

Stimulus – response questions

Item A

The sexual abuse of children is a widespread phenomenon and much of it happens in the context of the family. Sexual abuse can most easily be defined as the carrying out of sexual acts by adults with children below the age of consent (sixteen years old in Britain). Incest refers to sexual relations between close kin. Not all incest is sexual abuse. For example, sexual intercourse between brother and sister is incestuous, but does not fit the definition of abuse. In sexual abuse, an adult is essentially exploiting an infant or child for sexual purposes. The most common form of incest is one that is also sexual abuse – incestuous relations between fathers and young daughters.

Incest, and child sexual abuse more generally, are phenomena which have been 'discovered' only over the past ten to twenty years. Of course it has long been known that such sexual acts occasionally occur, but it was assumed by most social observers that the strong taboos which exist against this behaviour meant that it was not widespread. Such is not the case. Child sexual abuse is proving to be disturbingly widespread.

Source: A. Giddens, *Sociology*, Cambridge: Polity Press, 1989.

Item B

Child abuse – reported cases

In England and Wales the most systematic studies of this type have come from the research unit of the National Society for the Prevention of Cruelty to Children (NSPCC). Since 1974, cases of child abuse and suspected child abuse have been recorded on child protection registers. In a number of areas, covering almost 10.5 per cent of the population of England and Wales, these are controlled by the NSPCC. By careful examination of cases on their registers each year, the NSPCC is able to provide estimates of the levels of different types of abuse for England and Wales as a whole.

The NSPCC data suggest that in 1989 over 36,000 children in England and Wales were recorded as either having been abused or giving rise to 'grave concern' over their safety. This is an incidence rate of 3.35 per 1000 children. NSPCC records show a dramatic increase of around 30 per cent per year in recorded cases in the early and mid 1980s, levelling out in 1987–88, and increasing again in 1989. The most commonly recorded forms of abuse are physical injury and sexual abuse, but the largest proportionate increases between 1988 and 1989 were in neglect, emotional harm and grave concern cases. Most people feel that while the overall increase in registered cases in the 1980s may be because of an increase in child abuse, it is more likely to reflect the increased reporting as a result of greater public awareness of the problem.

Reported cases provide a readily available source of data on child abuse which has been professionally identified. However critics claim that reported cases understate the true incidence of the problem, as many cases of abuse may not be reported or recorded.

There is some evidence to suggest that reported cases may provide samples which are systematically biased and therefore of little value for projecting guidelines about child abuse in general.

Source: adapted from S. Taylor, 'Measuring child abuse' in *Sociology Review*, February 1992.

Item C

Rape profile

Definition: rape is penetration of the penis into the vagina of a woman against her will. Penetration of the anus or mouth of a women or a man against their will is termed 'indecent assault', as are most other sex crimes.

The main statistics below are from a sample of 1,236 London women. They were 62% of a random sample of 2,000 approached by researchers.

1 in 6 women have been raped

This does not include attempted rape or assault or attacks on children under 16. It does include married women raped by their husbands. Figures extrapolated from police reports give a figure of 1 in 4 for US women.

1 in 12 rapes are reported to the police

This compares with 1 in 4 of women who seek counselling from UK Rape Crisis Centres. In the US as a whole 51% of reported rapists are caught. 76% of those are prosecuted and 47% of that 76% are acquitted.

3 in 4 attackers are known to the victim

For rapes reported to the police the figure is much lower at around 1 in 2. Women are more likely to report a stranger to the police.

1 in 20 rapes are gang rapes

For rapes reported to the police the figure is much higher. 30% in Washington, 40% in the UK generally, 43% in Philadelphia, 47% in Malaysia and 50% in Toronto. Women are more likely to report gang rapes to the police.

1 in 2 rapes involve violence in addition to the rape

For rapes reported to the police the figure is nearer 4 in 5, since women are more likely to report violent rapes.

1 in 2 occur in the home of the rapist or the victim

This proportion is similar for rapes reported to the police in Memphis and Philadelphia in the US.

The figure is likely to reflect women's tendency to avoid dangerous situations *outside* the home.

The rapist who pays the rent

- Over 1 million children in the UK will be sexually assaulted or raped by age 15, many by members of their own family.

  - 1 in 3 families in Cairo is incestuous.

  - 1 in 4 US children will be raped or sexually assaulted by a trusted adult by age 15.

  - 1 in 10 married women in the UK has been forced, with violence, to have sex with her husband.

Item D

Jane is defined as schizophrenic. She is in perpetual reverie, her own little dream world, which consists of a game of tennis. It is a game of mixed doubles; she is the ball. Jane sits motionless and silent and eats only when fed. The adults in her family are in a state of conflict, her father and his mother ranged against her mother and her mother's father. The two halves of the family communicate only through Jane; she is the go-between. The strain eventually becomes too much for her and she escapes into her dream world. However, as her 'dream' shows, even in this world she cannot escape from the clutches of the family. The game of tennis symbolizes the interaction patterns in the family. With examples such as this,

Laing shows how the family can be a destructive and exploitative institution.

Source: adapted from R.D. Laing, 'The politics of the family', in M. Haralambos and M. Holborn, *Sociology: Themes and Perspectives,* 3rd edn, London: Collins Educational, 1991.

(a) Suggest two reasons for the increase in the number of children registered at risk by the NSPCC as shown in Item B. **(2 marks)**

(b) The data in Item C suggest that rape and sexual abuse are more widespread than crime statistics indicate. What explanations have sociologists offered for the extent of rape and sexual abuse in modern Britain? **(5 marks)**

(c) Using material from the items above and elsewhere, evaluate the relative importance of the various factors which led to child abuse being '"discovered" only over the past ten to twenty years' (Item A, lines 16–17).
(7 marks)

(d) Identify the two most commonly recorded forms of child abuse (Item B). **(2 marks)**

(e) Item D suggests that the family is a 'destructive and exploitative institution' (lines 16–17). To what extent is this argument supported by sociological evidence?
(9 marks)

7 Phenomenological approaches

Key ideas

- Small-scale micro study of families and households
- 'Actors'
- Roles
- Interaction
- Negotiation
- Responsibility
- Meaning and understanding
- Explaining the everyday and apparently 'trivial'
- The 'social construction' of marriage

Key figures

- Berger and Kellner
- Sandra Wallman
- Mansfield and Collard
- Charles and Kerr
- Peter Aggleton
- Finch and Mason

The theoretical approaches to families and households considered so far (in Chapters 2–6) have in common the fact that they apply value judgements to the family, whether these be positive (in the case of functionalism) or negative (as in the approaches of Marxism, feminism, radical psychiatry and Michel Foucault).

Phenomenological approaches do not directly take any position on whether the way we live in families today is good or bad. Rather they are interested in observing the day-to-day world of interaction in families and households in a non-judgemental way. In this sense, despite evolving from very different intellectual traditions, they adopt a stance towards the subject of investigation similar to that of positivist sociologists, who advocate objectivity and value freedom with the intention of studying society in as scientific a manner as possible.

The introduction to the previous chapter examined the distinction between structuralist (macro) and interpretive (micro) approaches in sociology. The

Figure 7.1 The two
sociologies

	Structuralist	**Interpretist**
Focus	Macro - large-scale study	Micro - small-scale study
Unit of analysis	Society	Interaction
Research	Social surveys, quantitative techniques	Qualitative, observational, in-depth techniques
Key theme	The role of the family in society in relation to other social instructions	What occurs in families and how family life, roles and responsibilities are negotiated and understood.

phenomenological approach clearly belongs within the latter tradition. It emphasizes the small-scale, detailed aspects of everyday life in families and households.

Morgan (1985) points out that in reality this dichotomy is not as clear cut as Figure 7.1 suggests. There are some studies of the family that are clearly structuralist in emphasis, and others that have an exclusively small-scale focus, but often the distinction is blurred, particularly in much recent work. Even Parsons, who is often identified as a structural-functionalist working in a macro-sociological tradition, examined child socialization and the stabilization of adult personalities – more 'micro' concerns – as part of his work on the family (see Chapter 3, pages 34–6). Issues raised by micro-sociological studies can often be linked to more structural issues such as gender, social class and ethnicity.

The interpretive approaches covered in this chapter draw upon a diverse range of intellectual traditions, including:

• symbolic interactionism,

• ethnomethodology, and

• conversation analysis,

all of which derive from the phenomenological tradition in sociology.

Look up the above terms in your textbooks or dictionaries of sociology and make brief notes on each.

A common feature of this approach involves taking the actor's point of view. The sociologist attempts to enter the subjective world of individuals in families and households rather than imposing his or her own interpretation of their experiences. For instance, a phenomenological sociologist would be likely to encourage a divorcée to explain her situation in as much detail as possible, rather than using statistics and related demographic details of divorce rates to hypothesize about why people divorce. It might be plausible to construct an explanation for rising divorce rates in terms of changes in legislation or the declining influence of religion, but such explanations would probably come from the sociologist rather than the divorcée.

Another feature of the phenomenological approach is that it turns away from the dramatic and unusual, and instead focuses attention on immediate and small-scale events, which can range from conversations at the breakfast table to everyday matters such as the preparation and eating of food.

Phenomenologists emphasize *meaning*: they conduct detailed examinations of what people say to unravel what they mean by it. For example, if a wife says, 'He's a good husband to me,' what does she have in mind?

- Does a 'good husband' bring her tea in bed once a year because it is her birthday?

- Does he do half the housework and childcare?

- Or does he never hit her, as her friend's husband hits his wife?

 Think of several statements about life in families similar to 'He's a good husband to me', and analyse them in terms of meaning as above. Work in pairs or small groups, and when you have finished report your examples to the rest of your class.

Associated with the interest in meaning is a refusal of the 'taken for granted'. This involves taking terms that more conventional approaches may see as self-explanatory, such as 'mother', 'father', 'child', 'daughter', 'grandmother', 'cousin' and 'step-parent', and treating that as problematic; that is, their meaning to the people involved is something that needs to be explained. Similarly, a phenomenologist may want to know 'how' or 'what' it is to 'do the work' (an ethnomethodological term) of being a 'mother', 'daughter' and so on.

Explain how the family terms 'aunt' and 'uncle' may sometimes be ambiguous.

The phenomenologists' focus on the 'how?' and 'what?' aspects of family life stands in sharp contrast to the 'why?' emphasis of other sociological approaches. Typical phenomenological questions are:

- How are relationships between husbands, wives and children in families negotiated and arranged?

- What is going on?

- How do we make sense of particular aspects of life in households?

If we take housework as an illustration, phenomenological sociologists would look at how this is negotiated and ordered within families and households and the associated meanings attached to such activities. As seen earlier (see pages 67–70), more traditional sociological approaches examine housework by focusing on issues such as:

- Why is most housework done by women?

and will provide answers such as 'Because we live in a patriarchal society' (feminism), 'Because this suits the needs of a capitalist society' (Marxism) or 'Because this suits the needs of an advanced industrial society' (functionalism).

Voysey (1975) investigated how parents with severely handicapped children used notions of 'normal' family life to cope with, and come to terms with, what to many outsiders might seem an abnormal, or certainly painful, domestic situation.

Think of some examples of how such a family may regard as 'normal' what outsiders would see as difficult or full of problems.

Another aspect of phenomenological approaches concerns methodology. A common feature of conventional sociological research is to create distance or detachment between observer and observed in order to establish objectivity, which is seen as essential for a scientific frame of reference. The assumptions are:

- that people give flawed or impartial accounts of their lives;

- that the feelings, views and values of the observer are separable from the analysis; and

- that the style, language and context of presentation all have to be observed with scientific detachment and rigour, excluding emotional feelings or reactions to the subject of study, for instance domestic violence.

Phenomenological studies, in contrast, involve an acknowledgement that there is interaction between the observer and the observed, and these interactions are central to the process of doing the research. Sociologists working in this tradition use 'softer', in-depth qualitative methods of research to elicit more *private*, detailed accounts than the *public* statements that are generally gathered by conventional survey research.

To illustrate the issues, consider research into the happiness of marriages. Social survey research using questionnaires may feature a question such as: 'Would you say your marriage is (a) Happy? (b) Reasonable? or (c) Unhappy?' To such an admittedly naive question most respondents would probably answer 'Happy' (a *public* response). Is this a real reflection of the state of marriage in contemporary society? Phenomenologists would doubt this, and suggest that questions about happiness or unhappiness in the *private* world of marriage require the use of more effective, qualitative research methods.

Consult the methodology/research methods sections of textbooks or your class notes to clarify the issues surrounding qualitative and quantitative methods of research.

Such issues are not just relevant to the study of marriage, families and households but are a feature of many topics in sociology. In practice much of the more recent research, including some of the studies mentioned in this chapter, combines quantitative and qualitative approaches in order to gain as full a picture as possible. This is sometimes referred to as triangulation or multi-method research.

Use textbooks to find examples of such studies.

An interpretive approach can also be applied to the more unusual or 'strange' aspects of daily interaction in families which may be puzzling and otherwise inexplicable to outsiders. Morgan (1991) gives the example of a woman, a man and a child sitting at a breakfast table. The woman says, 'I must remember to get some more marmalade,' and everyone laughs. An example from my own family concerns cranberry sauce, which always provokes laughter when anyone asks for it at a Christmas meal. The explanation is that twenty years ago the whole of my family was made ill by some pesticide-contaminated cranberry sauce, and the memory still produces an amused reaction.

> **1** *What would an outside sociological observer make of such a scene?*
>
> **2** *Think of an explanation of the 'marmalade' episode similar to the 'cranberry' story.*
>
> **3** *Can you think of any similar incidents, sayings or situations from your own family which would seem equally bizarre or strange to an outsider?*

Until fuller explanations are provided, much of daily life and interaction in families and households can seem puzzling. This is the essence of the phenomenological focus on meaning.

Critics say that such work and examples of study are trivial and should not be the concern of 'serious' scholarly research. Phenomenologists disagree and see such matters as the essence of social life which must be understood before the more structural links with issues such as gender, class or ethnicity can be made.

Phenomenological/interpretive research studies

This section takes a look at several examples of research within a phenomenological and interpretive framework to give a picture of the type of work being carried out.

Berger and Kellner (1964)

Peter Berger and Hansfried Kellner's essay 'Marriage and the construction of reality' is now regarded as a pioneering work in the field. They looked at marriage and the relationships, roles and interactions between husbands and wives from the point of view of meaning – what it is to be a husband or a wife, and how such behaviours are social constructions centred on mutual expectations, obligations and negotiations between marital partners. Berger and Kellner's approach is rooted in the sociology of knowledge, which is concerned with how our understanding of the world is socially constructed and in constant need of validation in interaction with others.

> *'Do you really love me?' may be seen as typical of the trivial everyday interaction between marital partners, but for Berger and Kellner such questions are very serious and reflect the precarious nature of our sense of social reality, which constantly needs reaffirmation.*
>
> **1** *Which marital partner do you think is likely to be saying this, and to whom?*
>
> **2** *What gender issues and related matters may be involved?*

Berger and Kellner's work laid the foundations for the phenomenological approach to the family and marriage. It is now worth considering a number of more recent studies to see how this tradition has developed. Close examination reveals that despite their interpretive emphasis in terms of research methodology and how the study is carried out, the work is often linked to macro-sociological concerns about power, authority and gender. As Morgan (1985) points out, the so-called 'gap' between the interpretive and structuralist approaches may not be as wide as is often assumed. Recent work on families and households covers a wide range of issues including how money is controlled, relationships between mothers and daughters, the family meal, adultery, TV viewing and responsibilities within families.

Wallman (1984)

Sandra Wallman's study entitled *Eight London Households* is a report of the final stages of a longer study concentrating, as the title suggests, on a small sample of households in South London. The sample included two single-parent households, two households of West Indian origin, two 'typical English' households and two households based on second marriages. It shows that even a small sample lends support to the 'diversity' argument presented in several sections of this book.

Members of each household were interviewed in detail about their daily lives, their past and present experiences of household organization, and how they coped with crises. They gave detailed job histories and filled in time charts that showed exactly how they spent their time over a given twenty-four-hour period. An interesting innovation in the study was the use of 'network maps', which looked at the people who were geographically close and those who were close in terms of affection or liking to see what sorts of resources they provided.

The households were based in the inner city, and its findings contradicted some of the assumptions commonly made about family life in such areas. In particular, one-parent and ethnic minority households are often stereotyped as 'problem' or 'difficult' families. In fact the two one-parent families, headed by West Indian mothers, managed very well despite financial difficulties and provided a stable and secure home supported through local networks close to the household, such as childminding for working mothers.

Mansfield and Collard (1988)

Penny Mansfield and Jean Collard's study, *The Beginning of the Rest of Your Life?*, focuses on the processes of becoming a married couple in a sample of first marriages, and goes on to explore the early years of marriage. The authors examined:

- living arrangements;

- how decisions were made about the division of labour in the home;

- how paid employment and domestic life were balanced;

- wives' and husbands' responses to conflicts and differences of opinion within marriage.

Mansfield and Collard used the in-depth interview, which they described as 'a conversation with a purpose'. Their aim was to develop something as close to natural conversation as possible. A total of 130 two- to three-hour interviews were carried out by an all-female research team with both marriage partners.

1 *What problems might be involved with such a research technique?*

2 *In the light of your knowledge of research methods and interview techniques, why do you think an all-female research team was used?*

Morgan (in Warde and Abercrombie 1994) points out in a review essay that small-scale qualitative studies of this kind do not produce 'findings' in the conventional sense, although some descriptive generalizations, such as the fact that over half the sample started their married lives in their own accommodation, can be linked to a discussion of the importance of starting out married life independently.

The study points to the dynamic processes of change and development that are part of married life and how these are not as predictable as implied in the sociological usage of the term 'career'. Behaviour and accepted patterns of interaction can shift and change through time. A common finding concerning the division of labour was a 'neo-traditional' pattern in which both partners are in paid employment but the female does most of the domestic labour while the husband 'helps' as necessary. This of course does not fully support the symmetrical family thesis (see pages 67–8). Traditional views of the greater importance of the husband's work were upheld; some couples had arrived at a sort of symmetrical understanding in that they expected a shared or balanced burden of household responsibilities despite housework being the majority task for wives.

 Discuss in pairs or make notes on this question: If housework is a 'majority task for wives', what are husbands doing in such homes that might represent 'a shared or balanced burden of household responsibilities'?

Another feature of the study was the identification of husbands and wives as 'Planners' and 'Non-planners', the latter being split into 'Venturers' and 'Roamers'. These could vary with partnerships, so a 'Planner' husband could be married to a 'Roamer' wife or a 'Roamer' wife married to a 'Venturer' husband. Attitudes in a Roamer wife–Venturer husband partnership are reflected in this quote: 'We didn't really plan – no definite date for the wedding – just see how it goes – drifted along I suppose. Andy got fed up on his own – so we decided to marry.'

This quote clearly indicates the phenomenological 'feel' of this research, which stands in clear contrast to more traditional quantitative methods. The interviewing technique gives respondents free rein to talk at will and disclose all important facets of the *how* and the *meaning* associated with behaviour that would not be dealt with in more rigid survey-type research.

Charles and Kerr (1988)

The nature of food and the family meal has received little attention from sociologists, but food is a very important aspect of family life, as Warde and Abercrombie (1994) affirm: 'Food habits tell a great deal about the texture of family relations, the generation and reinforcement of gender divisions in the household, and social distinctions between people belonging to different categories.'

Explain this statement, using appropriate examples.

Most British households spend approximately one-fifth of their budgets on food. Food preparation and family meals tell us a lot about key aspects of life in families and households. Communal eating and sharing food are sometimes central to the definition of a household.

In their study, *Women, Food and Families,* Nickie Charles and Marion Kerr used in-depth interviews with a sample of 200 women, each of whom had at least one pre-school child, so the sample was relatively young. As is typical in this sort of research, open-ended questions and verbatim responses were used as a basis for detailed qualitative data. In addition to the interviews, each respondent kept a diary recording what every household member ate and drank.

Charles and Kerr's findings pointed to the continuing tradition of the 'proper meal' – hot meat and vegetables at least once a day – and this was associated (in terms of meaning) with the 'proper family' and familial harmony. Family meals were also important features of the socialization of young children into accepted cultural habits and manners.

Food and family meals have strong emotional associations and are seen as important features of a happy family life. Class differences were evident, with the middle classes emphasizing the importance of taking the family meal at table, rather than while watching television.

Figure 7.2 The family meal

1 Why might the tradition of the family meal be considered important to familial harmony?

2 Explain the role of the family meal in child socialization, giving examples.

3 Why should there be a 'class' difference in the way the family meal is conducted?

On issues of gender differences it emerges overwhelmingly that women are the prime providers and preparers of food and meals, and this activity is invariably geared to the needs of their husbands and children. Women make a strong emotional investment in such matters, and consider it very important when meals are refused or a particular dish is not liked.

This study clearly shows the importance of food to family life, and it is an example of how research into what might be seen as trivial and mundane matters can in fact raise important sociological issues.

1 *Why might (a) the microwave oven and (b) different working times of parents affect the 'proper family meal' as described above?*

2 *Record details of when and how family meals are taken in your home throughout the week.*

Aggleton (1987)

Peter Aggleton's *Rebels Without a Cause* is a detailed observational study (an *ethnography*) of the sons and daughters of 'new middle-class' parents, that is, public sector professionals such as teachers and social workers. The subjects of study had 'rebelled' by failing or underachieving in their GCE A-Levels.

Data were collected over three years through a combination of participant observation and semi-structured interviews with twenty-seven students. Aggleton provides a very detailed portrait of the family life and households of the sample, referring to household size, types of furniture and decoration, state of tidiness/untidiness and related matters. In some households he even observed that pasta, rice and pulses were stored in jars and earthenware pans and dishes.

The research identified the families as 'left leaning', liberal households with a high degree of personal autonomy and negotiation of conduct between parents and children. The findings challenge more structuralist ideas of a straightforward link between class of origin and educational achievement as the students in the survey did not conform and rebelled against the demands of study and achievement. However, the author points out that other aspects of middle-classness – such as an antagonism towards working-class engineering students at college – were evident.

What other aspects of middle-classness may such 'rebels' retain?

Finch and Mason (1993)

Janet Finch and Jennifer Mason used a multi-method approach (see page 90) which included a large-scale survey as well as an in-depth qualitative study to consider whether families in contemporary western societies are becoming:

- smaller,

- more inward looking,

- less rooted in traditional kinship relationships, and

- less connected with other related families or the local community.

They focused on *obligations* – the way in which family members feel obliged to provide help and assistance to other family members. The qualitative part of the study looked at how beliefs (reflected in the survey data) translated into actual behaviour.

This study clearly shows the danger of oversimplifying from assumptions about the privatization of family life. Finch and Mason found that people still have an idea of family responsibilities and quite complex ways of negotiating and dealing with them. Rather than having detailed sets of rules about such matters, people more often subscribe to guidelines concerning reciprocity, the balance of independence and dependency, and related issues. These confirm how important and persistent family relations are in a supposedly isolated, privatized, inward-looking family world.

The phenomenological focus of this study is evident in its concern with issues of meaning in association with ideas about family responsibilities.

Consider the idea of 'responsibilities' as understood in your own family – for instance, when an older relative is ill – and note down examples of them. Use your observations in a class discussion of whether functionalist ideas about the 'isolation' of the nuclear family are correct.

Conclusion

This chapter has examined key aspects of the phenomenological approach to the family, which can be compared with structuralist approaches. To highlight the broad differences between the two traditions, let us look at criticisms that Morgan (1991) makes from a phenomenological perspective of an earlier structuralist study of divorce by Thornes and Collard (1979) which used a comparative survey of divorced and continuing married couples.

Morgan points out that there is a problem with retrospective accounts, which can be distorted by inaccurate recall. For example, in an interview a divorced man may want to reflect on his marriage experience and *restructure* it to fit in with his present situation by 'telling a story' that may not accurately reflect the way things actually were. So the aim of Thornes and Collard's research, to distinguish the 'divorce prone' from the 'less divorce prone', may not be achieved because of the possibly distorted findings on which the conclusions are based.

Another important issue from a phenomenological viewpoint concerns the meanings that people assign to divorce and marriage, which may be much more complex than Thornes and Collard's study recognizes.

The importance of interpretive approaches to the family lies in the way detailed attention to the 'micro' elements of the everyday world are addressed so that important issues of meaning, the 'how?' and 'what?' of family life, are uncovered – very much in the way archaeologists painstakingly piece together a picture of people's lives in the past. However, critics of the phenomenological approach raise a number of issues, two of which are methodological and one theoretical:

- Most of the studies described in this chapter are based on *small samples*, so there are difficulties associated with generalizing from their findings because the samples may be untypical. For instance, Charles and Kerr's study featured only young married couples with pre-school children, who may be unlike other families and households, such as those with adolescent children where behaviour patterns associated with food could be different.

Describe some of the differences that you might expect to find between such families.

- The close, *subjective* involvement of the researcher in the lives of the people studied might result in a distorted or overly sympathetic account of what is going on.

- Look up subjectivity in your textbooks and make notes on the methodological issues involved.

- Large-scale or macro issues of social class, gender and ethnicity that relate to the social structure may not be addressed.

In reply to the last point, it can be noted that a number of the studies featured in this chapter do raise such matters, albeit indirectly, rather than in the more critical manner that structuralist sociologists adopt. For example, feminists would want to make stronger links with issues of patriarchy and the wider social structure than are generally found in interpretive studies.

Despite such criticisms, it is noteworthy that much of the more recent empirical work on families and households has been within an interpretive framework, gathering important qualitative data that have significantly enhanced our understanding of families and households in modern societies.

Bibliography and further reading

Aggleton, P. (1987) *Rebels Without a Cause*, Basingstoke: Falmer Press

Berger, P.L. and Kellner, H. (1964) 'Marriage and the construction of reality', reprinted in M. Anderson (ed.) (1980) *Approaches to the History of the Western Family*, London: Macmillan

Charles, N. and Kerr, M. (1988) *Women, Food and Families*, Manchester: Manchester University Press

Finch, J. and Mason, J. (1993) *Negotiating Family Responsibilities*, London: Routledge

Morgan, D.H.J. (1985) *The Family, Politics and Social Theory*, London: Routledge

— (1991) 'The family', in M. Haralambos (ed.) *Developments in Sociology*, Vol. 7, Ormskirk: Causeway Press

Thornes, B. and Collard, J. (1979) *Who Divorces?*, London: Routledge

Voysey, M. (1975) *A Constant Burden*, London: Routledge

Wallman, S. (1984) *Eight London Households*, London: Tavistock

Warde, A. and Abercrombie, N. (1994) *Family, Household and the Life-Course*, Lancaster: Framework Press

Essay questions

'Concentrating on the trivial and everyday in families and households is the only way to ascertain a proper sociological portrait.' Examine this view.

Coursework suggestions

On pages 93–5 we looked at Nickie Charles and Marion Kerr's work, *Women, Food and Families*. Carry out similar research for one week in your own home. Write a short report for a class discussion.

This could be developed into a fuller piece of research by introducing comparisons with other households.

8   The New Right

'I work from the premise that the traditional monogamous marriage, with children, is in reality, on average, in the long run, the most satisfying way to live a human life.'

Charles Murray, *Sunday Times*, 22 May 1994

Key ideas

- The decline of the family
- Rising marital breakdown
- The attack on single parenthood
- Fatherless families
- Uncontrollable children
- Rising social problems and criminality
- Illegitimacy
- The 'underclass'
- The 'new rabble' and the 'new Victorians'
- A return to traditional values and the stable family

Key figures

- Charles Murray
- Brigitte Berger
- Abbott and Wallace
- Norman Dennis
- A.H. Halsey

The final theoretical approach that we shall be considering holds strongly to the view that the family has suffered a decline in comparison with the past. The nuclear family is seen as the most desirable environment in which to raise children. Anything else causes instability and social disorder, evidenced by increased social problems and crime among the young. A particular focus for New Right concern is the single-parent family.

New Right ideas first came to attention in the 1980s in both Britain and the USA. They have often been described as a conservative and right-wing philosophy and political outlook, linked to the monetarist economic policies pursued by the Thatcher and Reagan governments and to the religious fundamentalism of groups such as the Christian Right in America.

In fact New Right thinkers come from a range of disciplines, and include academics, journalists, philosophers and politicians as well as social scientists. The New Right approach is not a sociological theory as such, but its attitude to the family closely corresponds to that of functionalism (see Chapter 3) which sees the monogamous nuclear family as best 'fitting' the needs of a modern society.

One of the key figures associated with New Right sociological approaches to the family is Charles Murray, an American social scientist who has carried out research in Britain. His work came to public attention as a result of articles in the *Sunday Times* in 1989 and 1994. The Institute of Economic Affairs (IEA), described by critics as a right-wing think-tank, published his work in Britain as part of a series featuring titles attacking a number of aspects of modern life and times, such as:

- *The Family: Is It Just Another Lifestyle Choice?,*
- *Liberating Women . . . from Modern Feminism,*
- *Equal Opportunities: a Feminist Fallacy,* and
- *Rising Crime and the Dismembered Family.*

Such titles convey the flavour of New Right concerns – and illustrate why its critics describe the IEA as right wing.

Contrasting views on objectivity

According to the front covers of IEA publications, 'The Institute of Economic Affairs (IEA) is financed from a variety of private sources to avoid over-reliance on any single or small group of donors. All the Institute's publications seek to further its objectives of promoting the advancement of learning . . . the IEA has no corporate view.'

In the estimation of Professor Robert Moore, however, 'the [New Right] authors are deeply anti-egalitarian. Their work seems to be more ideological than scholarly' (in Abbott and Wallace 1992). Pamela Abbott and Claire Wallace add: 'The dominant influence in New Right thinking, in terms of images of the family, is the conservative one.'

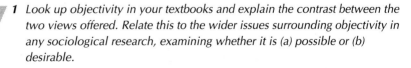

1 *Look up objectivity in your textbooks and explain the contrast between the two views offered. Relate this to the wider issues surrounding objectivity in any sociological research, examining whether it is (a) possible or (b) desirable.*

2 *Examine and make a list of the arguments for and against the view that Marxists and feminists can be objective in their approach.*

In opposition to critics of the nuclear family such as the Marxists, feminists and others whom we have met in earlier chapters, New Right thinkers seek to defend it against what they see as deteriorating social standards and left-wing attacks. The New Right is worried about a number of current trends in society:

- increasing permissiveness;

- sexual promiscuity;

- divorce and marital breakdown;

- increased cohabitation;

- a rising rate of illegitimate births; and

- increased numbers of single-parent families.

Such trends are seen as signs of moral and social breakdown, creating instability and disequilibrium. They are linked to:

- rising crime rates;

- juvenile delinquency and hooliganism;

- drug abuse;

- educational failure; and

- a 'dependency culture' that fosters fecklessness and indifference to employment.

The last point is particularly associated with the growth of the Welfare State, which is a favourite target for New Right attacks. Of especial concern are young working-class males who are unemployed and who do not take responsibility for their children and families.

Figure 8.1 Are today's young men feckless yobs?

Controversially in America it is young black males who have been the focus of such attention. In Britain this form of racism has been less overt and the focus has been on young inner-city dwellers who in several parts of the country, for instance Glasgow and the North East of England, are predominantly white.

The New Right sees state provision of welfare benefits as in some way interfering with the natural order of things in relation to family life, disturbing relationships between males and females and undermining the raising of children. Briefly the argument runs as follows:

Figure 8.2 Taming the 'natural' man.

- Men are 'naturally' aggressive, individualistic, selfish and promiscuous. A monogamous marriage with responsibility for a family curbs such instincts.

- Women who work instead of looking after their homes and children take jobs away from such young men.

- The Welfare State provides benefits that act as a disincentive to finding and/or keeping work.

- Fathers absolve themselves of their responsibility for their children and correspondingly are not financially 'attractive' to the mothers of such children.

- Children, particularly the males, have no father/male role model, so they grow up to run wild, and in later life act as irresponsibly as their fathers.

- Young men in such situations are drawn into the world of drugs and crime.

Evaluate each of the above propositions, through discussion in small groups if possible, in preparation for a class debate featuring arguments for and against them.

New Right solutions

The following policies are characteristic of the New Right's response to the problems it identifies:

- The traditional family should be encouraged and strengthened, since the best situation for children is to be raised by two loving, heterosexual married parents.

- Welfare benefits should not be so high as to be a disincentive to work.

- The male breadwinner role should be reinforced and supported so that young men develop a sense of pride and responsibility.

- Women should recognize this and take as their sole or main responsibility the care of their homes and families, particularly when they have young children.

- Community spirit and neighbourliness should be fostered as support mechanisms for the family. Crime could be reduced by Neighbourhood Watch Schemes, so fewer police would be needed and taxpayers' money would be saved.

Consider the above solutions to New Right concerns about the family and note down any difficulties or problems that you can identify.

Such solutions can seem to be grounded in 'common sense', and thus they have a certain logic and appeal, but they throw up a number of controversial issues. In particular, New Right thinking on the 'male role' is attacked by feminists as a backward step for women. The idea that employed women have 'stolen' jobs from men, who have some sort of 'natural right' to them, is one that can be refuted on a number of grounds. Working-class women have worked outside the home for centuries out of necessity, and their labour has been valuable both for their own families and for the economy as a whole. Today, for financial reasons alone, many women simply do not have the option of staying home, even if they want to. Furthermore, many women work in low-paid, low-status jobs such as cleaning, catering, office and shop work, which are unlikely to be attractive to the New Right's army of prospective male 'breadwinners'.

The writings of Charles Murray

As already noted, Murray is one of the key contributors to New Right thinking. He visited Britain in 1989 and 1994, and researched inner-city areas in a number of regions. He suggests that between his visits the 'crisis' in such areas deepened. He uses the concept of the *underclass* to describe the unemployed, impoverished, inner-city working class. He presents a familiar New Right portrait of social decay, promiscuity and illegitimacy, fatherless children, criminal and drug-abusing young males roaming devastated council housing estates creating law and order problems.

Despite the avowed scholarship, the use of evidence and the scientific aura that surrounds his work, Murray freely uses several clearly emotive and derogatory terms, not least of which is the controversial 'underclass'.

Look up 'underclass' in your textbooks and make notes on why the term is controversial, drawing in issues of race and ethnicity.

In one of his most recent articles Murray compares the illegitimacy rates of the 'New Rabble' (the underclass), who are the low-skilled working class, to those of the 'New Victorians', who are the upper middle class. He notes that the rates are, and probably will remain, much higher for the 'New Rabble'. It is obvious that Murray admires the 'New Victorians', whose sense of family responsibility, fidelity, loyalty and disciplined parenthood he praises.

Figure 8.3 Britain today: the growth of illegitimacy

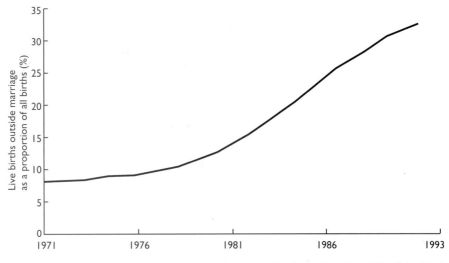

Source: *Office of Population Censuses and Surveys; General Register Office (Scotland); General Register Office (Northern Ireland)*

Murray cites studies of illegitimacy that link it with a range of social problems such as crime, drug abuse, prolonged unemployment and educational underachievement.

Take each of the above and find alternative explanations besides illegitimacy.

It is easy to stereotype Murray's writings as 'loony right-wing rhetoric', but closer examination reveals a depth of analysis and argument that merits consideration. Moreover, the views he propounds are not just the prerogative of the New Right, as we shall see in the next section.

Consider the following:

> 'Marriage,' it has been said, 'as an institution, is not fashionable in these districts.' And this is only the bare truth. Ask if the men and women living together in these rookeries are married, and your simplicity will cause a smile. Nobody knows. Nobody cares. Nobody expects that they are. In exceptional cases only could your question be answered in the affirmative. Incest is common; and no form of vice and sensuality causes surprise or attracts attention. Those who appear to be married are often separated by a mere quarrel, and they do not hesitate to form similar companionships immediately.

1 How do the views expressed in this quotation compare with the descriptions of the British 'underclass' given by Murray?

2 The description is from a nineteenth-century tract entitled The Bitter Cry of Outcast London. *What challenge does it offer to Murray and New Right thinkers concerning the deterioration of family life in the twentieth century?*

3 How can their views be seen as part of a 'Golden Age' approach?

Non-conservative support for New Right arguments

Brigitte Berger

In her essay 'The bourgeois family and modern society' (1993) and the book (co-authored with Peter Berger) *The War Over the Family* (1984), Berger argues that the institutions of modern society have common sources that are located in the individualistic familism of the 'bourgeois' family. Such a family is a central part of a modern society and in fact predates industrialization, so it is not, as used to be thought, a product of industrialization.

Berger cites various sources in support of this contention, including Peter Laslett and other historians (see pages 18–22) who have found evidence in England, France, Germany, Switzerland, Austria and North America that the Western nuclear family flourished long before the advent of industrialization. Berger goes further and suggests that the bourgeois family could have been the driving force behind industrialization: 'In fact, a good argument can be made that the bourgeois family has been the *only* institution sufficiently dynamic to engender the social processes making for both modernization and economic development' (Berger 1993, p. 9).

In the contemporary context Berger uses examples from Third World countries and Hong Kong to show how a strong form of family and associated networks in urban settings can be a vital buttress against poverty and an aid to economic survival.

> *How does Berger's view of 'Third World' inner-city families compare to the situation in British inner cities highlighted by Charles Murray?*

Leftist and Marxist critics tend to use the term 'bourgeois' in a negative sense, depicting a self-centred middle-class type of family that is obsessed with consumption and is unconcerned about the world beyond its immediate members. Berger rejects this view and sees the bourgeois family in a more positive light. She condemns the ideological overtones of Marxist views. She points to the public value of the bourgeois virtues of frugality, enterprise, decency, common sense, abstinence, discipline, reliability, politeness, respect for others and a general sense of fairness. She traces the roots of the word 'bourgeois' to ideas of civic duty and an intensified respect for individual rights.

> *How do the traits described by Berger compare with the qualities ascribed by Murray to his 'New Victorians'?*

Berger sees the left-wing ridiculing of the bourgeois family as part of the counter-culture of the 1960s, which increasingly focused on individuals and their needs and wants – a tendency sometimes referred to as 'atomized individualism' or in popular terms as the 'me generation'.

Berger also criticizes feminists, who have presented women in families as potentially autonomous individuals who can be isolated from their social circumstances of family, household, children and so on.

Theoretically, Berger can be associated with an interpretivist perspective as she is opposed to structural and systems approaches that see everything from the top down. She argues that we need to look at the everyday lives of human beings and how they live as individuals in families embedded in communal structures that give purpose to their actions and make sense of human life.

Berger's support for some of the views advanced by Murray and the New Right views emerges clearly in the following extract:

> . . . massive research demonstrates beyond the shadow of a doubt that by far the majority of ordinary people continue to be guided in their daily lives and their hopes for the future by bourgeois norms.
>
> The same body of research has made it evident as well, that a family consisting of a father and a mother, living together and being actively involved with the well-being and achievements of their children, is still the single best guarantee for an individual's success in school and in life beyond.
>
> (Berger 1993, p. 13)

Norman Dennis and A.H. Halsey

Dennis and Halsey are two eminent sociologists who describe themselves as 'Ethical Socialists', so they would clearly not subscribe to the political views of the New Right. Nevertheless, in turning their attention to issues of the family they have expressed similar concerns to writers such as Murray. Dennis's work has been published by the Institute of Economic Affairs.

In *Families Without Fatherhood*, Dennis and Erdos (1992) identified the rise in the number of children brought up without fathers as a worrying development. These children were invariably associated with antisocial behaviour, criminality, delinquency, educational underachievement and related social problems in greater proportions than their equivalent peers brought up in two-parent households.

This theme is taken further in Dennis's most recent work, *Rising Crime and the Dismembered Family* (1993), in which he further contends that such uncomfortable facts are glossed over or ridiculed by 'politically correct' 'conformist social affairs intellectuals' who treat such facts either as a reflection of a 'moral panic' or as evidence that the family is changing. In neither circumstance do these intellectuals see any cause for concern. Dennis, supported by Halsey, disagrees.

Dennis, Halsey and Berger, along with New Right thinkers, do not accept that the fragmentation of the family and the development of diversity in lifestyles and household structures are healthy social trends. They see the breakdown of the traditional nuclear family and its supportive network of kin – the modified extended family – as worrying developments leading to increased social problems.

These problems are particularly evident in inner-city areas and areas of high social deprivation such as the North East of England, South Wales, Manchester, Liverpool and Brixton in London. Such areas are predominantly lower or deprived working class, with high levels of unemployment and associated poverty. The contentious issue is whether fatherlessness and single parenthood on the one hand or unemployment and poverty on the other are the causes of the social problems found in such neighbourhoods.

In a lecture in Manchester in March 1994, A.H. Halsey admitted that the research so far has not managed to isolate either of the two key variables of poverty and single-parent (fatherless) families as *the* causal factor.

In a similar vein to criticisms of Murray's 'underclass' thesis, commentators point to the victimization or 'blame the poor' aspect of such arguments, but Halsey and others have produced evidence from across the social class spectrum that children in comparable social settings are at a disadvantage when brought up by one parent rather than two.

Furthermore, in support of Halsey, it could be suggested that, despite surface similarities between a single-parent and a dual-parent household in socio-economic terms, *qualitatively* the child's experience is different. Behaviour and school performance could be affected by tensions before and after divorce, unhappiness caused by feelings of rejection by the absent parent and dominant media images of happy two-parent families.

> *Consider the following two cases:*
>
> *1 A female doctor and a male doctor, married with children, divorce and the children remain with the mother.*
>
> *2 A female doctor and her manager husband, with children, remain married in a stereotypical nuclear family.*
>
> *Drawing on the arguments and counter-arguments mentioned in the last section, and adding your own ideas, make a detailed comparison of the lives you might predict for the children in the two families to support: (a) the view that the absence of the father results in difficulties for children, and (b) the argument that changed economic circumstances following divorce result in difficulties for families and children.*

Currently the picture is far from clear. New Right thinkers such as Murray as well as Ethical Socialists such as Halsey and Dennis highlight the lack of a father in a family. They consider this to be particularly bad for male children in deprived circumstances who have no adult breadwinner role model in their formative years. They grow up undisciplined and run wild in the streets.

Figure 8.4 A criminal of the future?

Murray refers to children as young as eighteen months playing out unsupervised in some inner-city areas. Such children have irregular or late bedtimes, which affects their school performance. For the New Right it is not surprising that crime and drugs become features of the lives of such children.

Controversy surrounding New Right approaches

Pamela Abbott and Claire Wallace (1992) criticize the New Right from a socialist-feminist perspective. The strong antagonism that some academics feel towards the New Right is epitomized in the Foreword to this book, where Professor Robert Moore remarks that Abbott and Wallace have 'plainly encountered modern authors whom they find hard to read with a straight face' (p. ix). Despite such reactions, however, New Right views have become increasingly politically acceptable and have regularly featured in the popular press and mass media.

Abbott and Wallace examine the work of a number of American and British academics and intellectuals whom they identify as key figures in New Right thinking. They trace the political links of such figures with Margaret Thatcher and Ronald Reagan, and their religious and moral connections with the Christian Right, especially notable with the anti-abortion lobby in America.

The core of New Right thinking, as we have noted, focuses upon the need for a strong nuclear family unit comprised of loving parents bringing up children. This, for sociologists echoing the views of Berger and the functionalists, is the core social unit that is essential for a stable, harmonious society, free from major social problems such as uncontrollable levels of crime. Implicit in this model is the figure of male breadwinner; his wife may perhaps work part time if they have children, but her main role is to feed and tend her husband and children, and to raise those children in a clean, ordered, stable and secure environment.

Abbott and Wallace believe that this is exploitative of women and that the New Right model covers up the degree of unhappiness and frustration experienced by many women in such circumstances, evidenced by the high incidence of illnesses such as depression among housewives. They also emphasize the extent and seriousness of violence perpetuated by husbands on wives and children (see pages 79–81), which does not seem to be recognized by the New Right.

Adherents of the Moral Right prefer to focus on issues such as illegitimacy and cohabitation, and are especially hostile towards feminist ideas such as the 'right to abortion'. They see such matters as threats to harmony and stability in society and as features of moral breakdown that must be strongly opposed. In extreme cases such opposition may include the use of violence: in 1993 two abortion clinic doctors were shot dead in America by anti-abortion campaigners, and since then there have been several similar attacks.

The New Right's concerns can be summarized as follows. They are for:

- home-making and childcare as the key elements of a woman's role;
- stability for children, reinforced by appropriate role models of a breadwinner father for boys and homemaker mother for girls;

> ## Ideas that become policy
>
> When Charles Murray first suggested abolishing welfare a decade ago, the concept was so radical that even he hardly dared believe it might become American government policy. In arguing that single mothers should be left to fend for themselves without state benefits, he was, he wrote, simply conducting a 'thought experiment'.
>
> But American politicians, both right and left, have grasped his ideas with enthusiasm. So mainstream has he become in America's welfare debate that President Clinton praised a recent Wall Street Journal article by Murray on the white underclass as 'essentially right'.
>
> Murray's philosophy is partly reflected in Clinton's current proposals to make people work for benefits – a move described by The New York Times as the 'toughest in the welfare system's half-century history'.
>
> *Sunday Times*, 29 May 1994

- all children to be brought up at home by two loving, heterosexual, married parents.

They are against:

- egalitarianism, since they believe that there are fundamental differences between men and women that determine what roles they are fitted for;

- easy availability of divorce;

- cohabitation, which they view as a sign of instability and impermanence;

- abortion, since they hold that foetuses have a 'right to life';

- feminism, which they hold responsible for unhappiness and the disruption of family life;

- one-parent families;

- homosexuality, which they believe to be 'deviant' and a sign of moral decadence.

> *Consider these lists of the New Right's concerns. Debate in class some of the issues that they raise, or do some research and make detailed notes on each of them.*

Abbott and Wallace take issue with all of the above positions. They favour tolerance and diversity in the way people live together, and recognize a variety of unconventional options that may be open to individuals during the course of their lives, including:

- living alone,

- living as homosexual couples,

- single-parent families,

- female breadwinners with househusbands caring for children,

and a range of other arrangements that do not conform to the pattern of the stereotypical nuclear family.

Conclusion

Of all the approaches, theories and perspectives we have examined so far, the views associated with the New Right perhaps arouse the strongest emotional responses. Given the topics covered in this chapter, this is not very surprising, particularly if one is a feminist, homosexual or Marxist. New Right views are not 'dry' academic debates divorced from the real world. They strike at the core of people's identities, feelings and self-esteem in ways that can provoke strong reactions.

The question arises as to whether it is possible to be scientific, detached, impartial and objective, and to conform to other conventions of academic debate, when considering issues that touch our personal lives so closely.

Considering some of the examples of New Right thinking described in this chapter, discuss in pairs why it might be difficult to preserve academic objectivity when studying the sociology of the family.

Bibliography and further reading

Abbott, P. and Wallace, C. (1992) *The Family and the New Right*, London: Pluto Press

Berger, B. (1993) 'The bourgeois family and modern society', in J. Davies (ed.) *The Family: Is It Just Another Lifestyle Choice?*, London: Institute of Economic Affairs

—— and Berger, P. (1983) *The War Over the Family*, London: Hutchinson

Dennis, N. (1993) *Rising Crime and the Dismembered Family*, London: Institute of Economic Affairs

—— and Erdos, G. (1992) *Families Without Fatherhood*, London: Institute of Economic Affairs

Essay questions

Assess the view that the decline of marriage and the rise of the single-parent household threaten the stability of society.

Coursework suggestions

Carry out an investigation among your fellow students, relatives and neighbours, using questionnaires and interviews, to explore how some of the ideas of the New Right are viewed by your respondents. The hypothesis you will be testing is that New Right approaches to the family accurately reflect popular opinion.

9 Marital stability and divorce

'Those whom God hath joined together, let no man put asunder'.

Key ideas

- Romantic love
- Monogamy
- Arranged marriage
- Cohabitation
- Secularization
- Divorce
- Exogamy
- Endogamy
- 'Empty shell' marriages
- Privatization of the family
- Effects of divorce on children
- Serial monogamy

Key figures

- Coleman & Salt
- Hollinger & Holler
- Margaret Mead
- Jesse Bernard
- Nicky Hart
- Young & Wilmott
- Paul Bohannan

Marriage refers to the public affirmation of a loving relationship between an adult male and female in a civil or religious ceremony (a wedding) for the purpose of a faithful lifelong sexual and social partnership and the raising of children. Further than this we can note the following features:

- In Western societies choice of marital partner is based on 'falling in love' (romantic love), whereas in many other societies choice of partner is determined among the wider family and kin (the arranged marriage).

- In Britain, patrilineal descent (the passing of inheritance and property through the male line) is symbolized by the wife taking her husband's surname prefixed by Mrs, so Miss Smith might become Mrs Jones.

- The newly married couple will generally take up residence separately from their families of origin in a 'neo-local residence' – that is, in a new location, often near their parents, though they may move to another area.

- Until recently the system of patriarchy was reinforced in the marriage vow, in which the wife promised to 'love, honour and *obey*' her husband. The husband did not make this promise to his wife. In recent times the choice of the promise to 'love, honour and *cherish*' for both partners has been offered as an alternative.

Is this change of wording a reflection of more egalitarian times?

A careful reading of relevant sections of this book, for instance on the debate about the isolation of the nuclear family (see pages 21–3), will help you to examine these features of contemporary marriage critically, answer the following questions and explain your answers:

1 Does every heterosexual couple forming a stable monogamous relationship affirm their intention so to do in a public ceremony, i.e. a wedding?

2 Are monogamy and the associated ideal of fidelity to one person for life consistently observed?

3 Do all married couples eventually raise children?

4 Is choice of marital partner a random and mysterious affair, as in the song lyric, 'Some enchanted evening, you may see a stranger across a crowded room'? What part do social class, race or ethnicity, culture, religion and age play in one's choice of partner?

5 What proportion of marriages last 'until death us do part'?

6 Has the extended family become unimportant?

7 Do all wives take their husbands' surnames?

8 Are traditional patriarchal ideas of wives serving husbands still relevant in a modern society?

Your answers to such questions should illustrate the complexity of current trends.

In Britain the majority of people still marry, but in the last decade a number of developments have been taken as signs that marriage is declining in popularity. The marriage *rate* (the numbers of people who marry per head of the marriageable population) has declined, leading some commentators to predict that in the next century marriage may become a minority experience. Questions then arise as to what may be taking its place.

Current trends in marriage around the world

Giddens (1993) agrees with William J. Goode (1963) that in general there is a trend

Figure 9.1 Changing world patterns in marriage and family life

Social organization/ ideology	Patriarchy/ matriarchy	⇨	Egalitarian
Family type	Extended	⇨	Nuclear, symmetrical
Number of partners	Polygamy	⇨	Monogamy
Partner choice	Arranged	⇨	Romantic love
Treatment of children	Sent to work at an early age	⇨	Protected and nurtured
Role of children in	Producers	⇨	Consumers
Domestic labour	Female	⇨	Shared

towards adopting Westernized forms of marriage and family structure. Change is occurring in a number of directions (see Figure 9.1):

1 Clans and other corporate kin groups are declining in influence. In China the old Tsu system of kinship and land-holding was abolished after the establishment of Communism in 1949, giving way to more nuclear-style family structures which are considered appropriate to an era of industrialization and modernization.

Figure 9.2 Chinese nuclear family

2 There seems to be a general trend towards a free choice of spouse in line with the concept of romantic love, accompanied by a decline in arranged marriages. Extended families are usually associated with arranged marriages, and these too have declined in influence.

3 The importance of kinship groups in determining choice of marriage partners is declining. Both *endogamy* (marriage within one's own kinship group) and *exogamy* (marriage outside it) are giving way to the desire of individuals to choose whomever they wish.

4 There is a trend towards egalitarian marriage. Increasing rights for women have been reflected in their greater choice of marriage partner and greater freedom within the marriage, reflecting a shift in the balance of power within the relationship.

5 Greater sexual freedom associated with the availability of more reliable birth control means that sexual experience is now much more widely available and may even be expected before marriage. This connects with the increasing popularity of the notion of sexual compatibility and an aspiration to a 'healthy' sex life within marriage – trends backed up by an army of 'experts', such as doctors, counsellors and advice columnists, and a deluge of information in the mass media (as we noted in our examination of the work of Michel Foucault, pages 81–3).

The notion of sexual experience prior to and sexual compatibility within marriage are very much twentieth-century developments. In earlier times the virginity of the bride (but not the husband!) was seen as essential, even to the extent that it sometimes had to be faked because if the bride was not, or appeared not to be, a virgin on the wedding night the marriage would be jeopardized.

1 Take each of these five points in turn and discuss in more detail the trends they claim to identify, drawing upon appropriate sections of this book and your textbooks.

2 Can you find any evidence that any of these trends is not occurring? If so, explain your findings.

Giddens notes that each of these trends can be exaggerated; there are differences in the speed at which such developments are occurring, and there are some reversals and counter-trends. In Poland, for example, Höllinger and Haller (1990) note a revival of the extended family, with grandparents moving in to help with the running of a household and children while the parents go out to work. There is also evidence in Britain of the continuing involvement of grandparents in childcare for working parents, a role that may grow as more people take early retirement and in general are living longer, healthier and more active lives.

Marriage in Britain and Europe

The state of marriage in Europe offers a somewhat mixed picture. There are generalized signs of a decline in marriage in a number of countries, notably in Scandinavian ones such as Denmark and in the United Kingdom, whereas in contrast

Table 9.1 Marriages, an EU comparison 1981–9

Marriages per 1,000 eligible population

	1981	1989
United Kingdom	7.1	6.8
Belgium	6.5	6.4
Denmark	5.0	6.0
France	5.8	5.0
Germany (Fed. Rep.)	5.8	6.4
Greece	7.3	6.1
Irish Republic	6.0	5.0
Italy	5.6	5.4
Luxembourg	5.5	5.8
Netherlands	6.0	6.1
Portugal	7.7	7.1
Spain	7.7	7.1

Source: Statistical Office of the European Communities

marriage continues to enjoy great popularity in countries such as Ireland, Italy and Spain.

Research using library sources and list factors that might explain such differences.

Coleman and Salt (1992) suggest that in Britain there has been considerable erosion of traditional assumptions and attitudes such as that:

- marriage confers on a woman a secure, settled income and a status and role based on raising children and keeping house, tasks around which most of the rest of her life will revolve;

- marriage lasts for the rest of an increasingly long life; and

- marriage is the setting for almost all childbearing and sexual cohabitation.

These beliefs are being challenged and changed by:

- new ideas;

- new economic roles for women;

- new laws; and

- family planning.

Take each of these changes in turn and explain them in more detail, giving appropriate examples.

Cohabitation

One of the key trends since the late 1980s in countries such as Denmark, Britain and France is the rise in the numbers of cohabiting couples. In the mid–1980s it was estimated that there were 900,000 cohabiting couples in Britain, bringing up 400,000 children; these numbers have continued to grow and the trend is predicted to continue.

Cohabitation is not a new phenomenon, however. There is historical evidence (see Chapter 2) that cohabitation has always been an option for a significant number of couples. Marriage, as currently recognized in terms of a religious ceremony, was not widely available to the majority until the nineteenth century. It was then that terms such as 'living in sin' and 'living over the brush' (thought to be derived from an old custom of a couple jumping over a broom to signify their union) came to be commonly used as derogatory terms, because previously it was socially acceptable to live together and be seen as 'married' without any formal religious or similar ceremony.

The older generation (ask your grandparents!) may still show mild disapproval and use terms such as 'living in sin' for younger cohabiting couples in their neighbourhood.

> *Look up the term 'common law', in the context of common-law marriage, common-law wife or common-law husband. What does it mean? Search newspaper articles for the term. In what context does it appear and what stereotypes are involved in its usage?*

The changing nature of cohabitation

Until relatively recently, sociologists and social scientists saw cohabitation as a temporary phase within the life cycle of a couple prior to eventual marriage. For example, students might cohabit at university and marry when their careers were established. A significant factor would usually be pregnancy and forthcoming parenthood (to avoid the stigma of illegitimacy), but social pressures from older relatives could play a part.

Family ways

Keen Westminster-watchers will be eagerly debating whether the first signs of the end of silly season and the advent of party conference season (a subtle but significant distinction) have arrived. Once again the family is the target of muddled thinking and inappropriate moral interference.

Social Security Minister, Alistair Burt, has condemned trends in cohabitation for contributing to the growing instability of the family. He has cited research which he says indicates cohabiting couples being four times more likely to split up as married couples. Such statistics need to be treated with the utmost caution. Cohabiting couples inevitably include a much greater diversity of relationships than might be expected within a marital union, and many of those who cohabit do so (and expect to do so) for a relatively short period.

The real comparison has to be between married and cohabiting couples *who have children*, and here the picture is likely to be far less black and white. Alistair Burt is right, of course, to emphasize that children need to be brought up in warm, loving and secure relationships, but it is premature to conclude that this is more likely to be found in a married relationship.

Alongside the rise in cohabitation has been another, less publicised trend, which has seen the increasing tendency for births outside marriage to be registered by both parents. In 1981 this was true of around 58 per cent of such births. Ten years later it was the case with around three quarters. Most of these parents share the same address. Joint registration is a deliberate choice, and might be viewed therefore as an important indicator of some commitment to parental responsibility, and to the cohabiting relationship which in many instances will be indistinguishable from marriage.

Interpreting complex trends in the changing nature of family life is a difficult business, and one where simplistic conclusions are to be avoided. Certainly we need to know the consequences of different types of family formation for the well-being of children, but such evidence is complex and often contradictory.

It is unfortunate that the real debate which does need to take place about major family policy issues has once again been distorted by moral panic and an inappropriate belief in the capacity to resurrect the traditional family.

Melanie Henwood (Social policy analyst).
Source: *Guardian* 16 September 1994

1 *Why does Melanie Henwood say the statistics of breakdown in cohabiting relationships needs to be treated with caution?*

2 *What evidence does she use to show that there seems to be growing stability in cohabiting relationships?*

3 *What is a 'moral panic' and how does this relate to the family?*

4 *What type of family would (a) Alistair Burt and (b) Melanie Henwood favour?*

Margaret Mead, an American anthropologist, used the term 'trial' or 'probationary marriage' to describe the phase of cohabitation during the marital life cycle. However, the view that cohabitation is a temporary condition is changing in the light of more recent evidence of permanent cohabitation among ever-larger numbers of couples, indicating that there has been some sort of attitude change.

Mead suggested that in the future there is no reason why each of the stages 1 to 5 shown in Figure 9.3 should not be with a different partner. What would this be called? Do you agree that this may happen? Explain.

Unfortunately, precise evidence on cohabitation as compared to marriage is difficult to obtain. In Britain the Office of Population Censuses and Surveys has accurate records of marriage numbers obtained from Registrars who have to complete and forward details of every marriage. People receive a Marriage Certificate as proof of their status. There is no equivalent in a cohabiting relationship, so evidence of a more interpretive kind has to be used.

One such piece of evidence has been the rapid rise in Britain of births of babies with

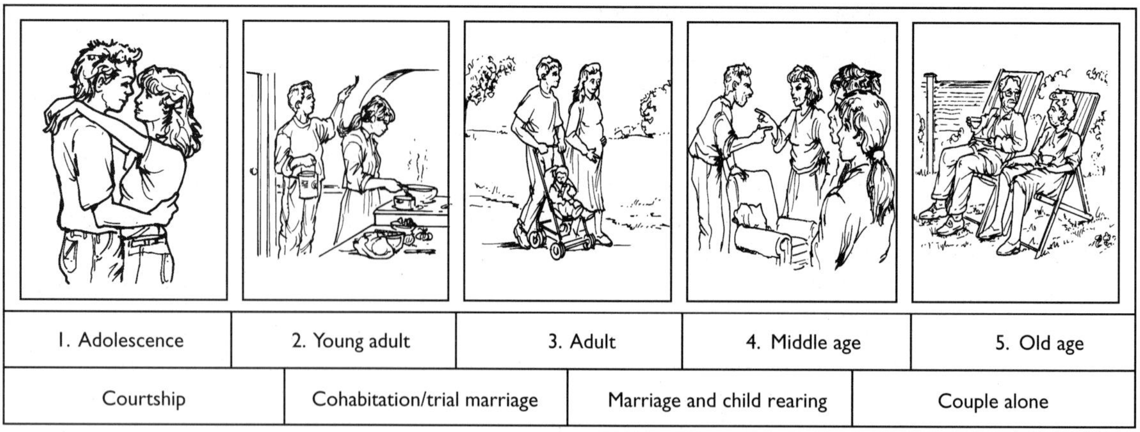

1. Adolescence	2. Young adult	3. Adult	4. Middle age	5. Old age
Courtship	Cohabitation/trial marriage	Marriage and child rearing		Couple alone

Figure 9.3 Margaret Mead's family life cycle

unmarried parents, currently around 32 per cent or almost one-third of the total births compared to around 5 per cent in the early 1960s. Another significant piece of evidence is that the majority of such births are registered by both parents living at the same address. This leads commentators to suggest that lifelong cohabitation has become an alternative choice to lifelong marriage for increasing numbers of couples.

The following explanations of the rise in cohabitation have been offered:

- Social attitudes: attitudes and values concerning marriage have changed, and the institution is seen as less important than it was.

- Economic factors: the cost of the average wedding can be in excess of £5,000; a wedding dress alone can cost up to £1,000. Rising unemployment, economic instability and escalating costs of housing may lead people to question the necessity of expenditure on a wedding.

Conduct a survey of the total costs of a traditional wedding in your area, making a list of items and services generally considered necessary, such as the dress, transport and the reception, and pricing them through appropriate shops, advertisements and other agencies.

- Employment trends: instability in employment and job prospects may make people wary of committing themselves to long-term relationships. This may particularly apply to young males who have little chance of finding a job and fulfilling the role of 'breadwinner' (see page 100).

- Religious trends: the influence of religion in British society is declining (a phenomenon known as secularization). Around 10 per cent of the population now attends church regularly. Religion is not the main focus of many people's lives, so underpinning marriage with a religious service is less likely to seem necessary than it once did.

- Rising divorce rate: cohabiting couples may have experienced the divorce of their parents and may not wish to risk the same experience themselves. There is an increased awareness of divorce as a result of messages from family, friends, the mass media and a wide range of social sources which highlight the suffering and pain involved.

The future of cohabitation

Some commentators point out that cohabiting relationships are less stable than marriages. A 1994 Economic and Social Research Council report found that couples living together were four times more likely to separate than married couples. However, this study did not distinguish between couples with and without children, so a wide range of circumstances could be aggregated together in the results. Some types of cohabitation – such as when students live together – can be expected to be short-lived. On the other hand, five out of six parents who separate with children living at home are married, but of course this proportion could be expected since the majority of parents are married.

> There is a belief, especially among the older generation, that marriage is inherently a more stable institution, as reflected in the comment: 'If you're married you have to work at it. Living together isn't the same – you could have a row or something and one of you could just walk out.'
> Debate the merits of this viewpoint and make notes giving more detail as to why the speaker believes marriage to be more stable than cohabitation. Do you agree? If not, give your reasons.

As we have noted, not all European countries have high levels of cohabitation: those with a strong religious tradition such as Ireland, Spain and Italy still have high marriage rates. This may change, however, as modernizing trends such as urbanization and the growth of secular culture undermine traditional ways of life, leading the younger generation to break away from the extended family and encouraging them to experiment with other forms of relationship such as cohabitation.

Arranged marriages

In Britain this type of marriage is often associated with South Asian communities. Most of these are Muslim; others are from a Hindu or Sikh background.

Non-Asian outsiders often have a stereotyped and negative image of arranged marriages, featuring a Westernized adolescent girl being forced against her will to marry a complete stranger. In more traditional communities with strong cultural codes there have been some cases where a female born and educated in Britain undergoes an arranged marriage to someone she has not met until just before the ceremony. It may be that an arranged marriage in these circumstances would cause unhappiness because of her experience of two cultures – that of her family and ethnic background (where arranged marriage is the norm) and that of the Westernized wider society (where notions of romantic love prevail).

Evidence of the difficulties for some young Asian women of arranged marriages can be adduced from the suicide rate among young Asian females in Britain, which is three times that of equivalent non-Asian females. However, this figure should be treated with some circumspection, since it raises issues such as whether coroners subscribe to stereotypes of the Asian community which include ideas about the repressive nature of arranged marriages; this might make them more willing to deliver suicide verdicts.

Figure 9.4 An arranged marriage

Do you agree with this last point? Consult your textbook on the sociology of suicide to find out more about the controversy over suicide statistics and the role of coroners' definitions.

Are arranged marriages changing?

There is evidence that the arranged marriage based solely on familial duty is declining and that increasing numbers of young British Asians now have more choice and say in their marriages. A young woman can be introduced to a number of 'family-approved' prospective husbands, and she has the chance to refuse and negotiate with her parents until she meets a young man who is to her liking. However, her eventual marital partner is still usually of a similar background in terms of his religion and country of ancestry.

However, some Asian groups, such as Asians originating from West Africa, have more Westernized attitudes and accept inter-ethnic partnerships and romantic love as the basis of choice of marital partner. Such examples show the difficulty of over-generalizing about the Asian ethnic minority communities. The term 'Asian' covers a variety of cultural backgrounds which can differ widely according to:

* religion – whether Hindu, Muslim, Sikh or Buddhist;

- country of origin – from Africa, Bangladesh, India, Kashmir, Pakistan or elsewhere;

- length of residence in Britain – people who have arrived in recent years tending to have more traditional outlook than second- or third-generation residents;

- rural or urban origins – the former being associated with more traditional ways;

- social class – with more Westernized attitudes to marriage being associated with higher social class, occupational status, income and wealth, and educational qualifications (for example, the African Asian business and managerial class).

Taken as a whole, however, young British Asians have more choice and say than did previous generations. Their current situation is probably not dramatically different from that of young non-Asian adults who, while choosing their marital partners on the basis of romantic love, often marry people very similar to themselves in terms of background factors such as social class and educational qualifications. Parental influence may be less direct than in an arranged marriage, but parents can show disapproval of 'inappropriate' boyfriends or girlfriends.

> *Imagine that the daughter of two solicitors brings home a working-class boyfriend whom her parents deem 'unsuitable'. After he has left they remark: 'He's a nice young man, but not your type, darling. What happened to Simon, Doctor Jones's son who went to Oxford? Why don't you write to him?'*
>   *Compare this scenario with the likely course of an arranged marriage discussed above.*

A final point about arranged marriages is to compare the one in three divorce rate for marriages based on romantic love with the low divorce rate prevalent in Asian communities. It could be argued that couples embarking on an arranged marriage may have more realistic expectations than those who are marrying for love. Supporters of arranged marriages might claim that love is something that develops with time in such a relationship, whereas romantic love is likely to change into something less exciting, or disappear altogether.

Perhaps, therefore, relying on romantic love as the sole basis for choice is not such a good idea? However, it is well to be wary of drawing conclusions from a simple comparison of divorce rates. The complexities and issues involved will be examined in more detail in the next section.

> *Hold a discussion of the pros and cons of arranged marriage after you have conducted some further research. If you are Asian by background or have Asian students in your class, bring in the experiences of families in the local community who have arranged their marriages.*

Hindus seek love matches

Attitudes towards arranged mariages are changing very rapidly in Britain, according to a new study.

A survey of 107 Hindus and Sikhs aged between 16 and 25 born in Britain found that 60 per cent reject an arranged marriage and want to marry the person they fall in love with. 12 per cent of their parents had a love marriage.

The 40 per cent who accept an arranged marriage say they now have the chance to meet their prospective partners and have the final decision on whether the marriage will go ahead. Traditionally, the future couple met the day of their wedding.

The survey, The Great Leap, carried out by Dr Colin Francome, reader in medical sociology at Middlesex University, also revealed that 62 per cent of the women interviewed planned not to marry until after their 25th birthday. Their mothers were born outside Britain and nearly half married in their teens.

Young women are much more tolerant of children born outside wedlock than their mothers would have been; 70 per cent found such behaviour acceptable. Young men are not so tolerant, 51 per cent approved.

Two-thirds agreed with having sex with a future marriage partner but a double standard remained with men believing they were entitled to casual sex while women must keep to higher sexual standards. Young Hindus and Sikhs are moving rapidly away from traditional mores: nine in 10 found drinking alcohol acceptable and two-thirds said they would eat meat. Half did not attend religious services regularly.

Guardian, 25 June 1994

Divorce

Divorce rates in many societies throughout the world are high. This phenomenon is not confined to Westernized societies: Russia and the former Communist East European countries have very high rates.

A country with one of the world's highest divorce rates is the USA, where in one state – California – more than one in two marriages ends in divorce. Many see this as the way things are going in the rest of the world. However, in Europe some countries presently have low divorce rates, notably Italy, Portugal and Spain. (See Table 9.2, p.123)

> *Explain these low divorce rates. What factors may lead to an increase in divorce in these countries?*

Britain has one of the highest divorce rates in Europe, alongside Denmark. Figures from the nineteenth century show a long-term rise in the incidence of divorce. There are now larger numbers of divorced couples than at any previous time. A simple explanation would be that the population has increased, but examination of the divorce *rate*, which is the number divorcing per 1,000 married couples, also shows a dramatic rise.

The numbers of divorces per year have remained fairly constant in Britain since the early 1980s, which might be thought to represent a halt in the trend. However, we must not overlook the fall in the popularity of marriage and the rise in cohabitation that we noted in the previous section.

Table 9.2 Divorce: a worldwide comparison

	Marriage per 1000	Divorces per 1000
Australia	7.1	2.5
Austria	4.7	2.0
Belgium	5.8	2.0
Canada	7.1	2.4
Denmark	6.3	2.8
Finland	5.3	2.0
France	4.9	2.0
West Germany	6.5	2.1
Greece	5.2	0.9
Iceland	5.2	2.2
Ireland	5.1	–
Italy	5.5	0.5
Japan	5.8	1.3
Luxembourg	5.5	2.0
Netherlands	6.1	1.9
New Zealand	7.5	2.5
Norway	5.2	1.9
Portugal	7.0	0.9
Spain	5.3	0.5
Sweden	5.2	2.3
Switzerland	6.8	1.8
Turkey	7.6	0.4
UK	6.7	2.9
USA	9.7	4.8

Causes of divorce

Changes in legislation

The most commonly cited reason for the rise in divorce in the twentieth century is changes in the law which have gradually liberalized divorce, making it more easily obtainable for large numbers of people. There have been a number of significant Divorce Acts through the nineteenth and twentieth centuries, but probably the most significant in the post-war period is the Divorce Reform Act passed in 1969 and brought into effect in 1970.

> *The statistics (see Figure 9.5 on the next page) show a dramatic and steep rise in divorces in the years following the passage of the Divorce Reform Act. Part of the explanation may be a 'backlog' effect (as people waited to divorce until after the Act was passed), but think of other reasons why the Act may have encouraged divorce.*

The Divorce Reform Act was significant in that it qualitatively changed the grounds for divorce from 'matrimonial offence' to 'irretrievable breakdown' of a marriage. Previously divorce cases centred around one partner proving the matrimonial guilt of the other in a divorce court setting very much like a criminal court. 'Charges' of adultery, cruelty or desertion would be made by one partner against another.

> *Who do you think usually made the charge against whom? Explain.*

Figure 9.5 Divorce – trends since 1861

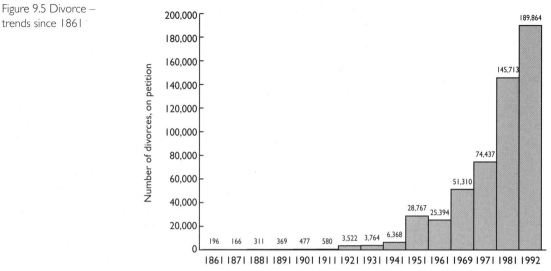

Such 'charges' had to be proved. If adultery was denied or contested, the spouse making the allegation would often hire a private detective to follow and collect evidence of the other's compromising behaviour. The 'seediness', stress and invasion of privacy entailed by this procedure led to pressure for the change to irretrievable breakdown as the key grounds for divorce.

Some of the previous grounds for divorce, such as adultery, can still be cited, but the Divorce Reform Act introduced the idea of *separation*. Separation can be accepted as sufficient grounds for divorce:

• after a period of two years if both partners agree, or

• after five years without mutual agreement.

Describe the circumstances of a couple for whom divorce may be agreed after two years, and another for whom it takes five years.

Introduction of the criterion of separation meant that, even where the former categories of 'guilt' such as adultery applied, there was an opportunity to opt for less 'messy' divorce proceedings after two years' separation.

Carry out research in the library to make a list of key Divorce Acts since the nineteenth century. Make notes on each. Compare the effects of each by looking at Figure 9.5 and noting rises in the numbers of divorces in the following years.

Changed attitudes

Following on from the effects of legislation outlined above, an associated factor is the increased acceptance of divorce in society. Divorce no longer carries the stigma that it did in previous times. The newspapers and television carry frequent stories about the separation and divorce of couples, often media stars and entertainers, and most notably members of the British Royal Family.

> *Why is the term 'Royal Family' somewhat ironic?*

Contact with divorce within families, among relatives, friends and neighbours is an increasingly common experience for many people.

> *Examine the amount of experience of and contact with divorce among your class or a small group of acquaintances to see how true this statement is for you.*

However, widespread familiarity with divorce does not necessarily mean that there is now an easygoing attitude towards it. Research indicates that divorced people can still feel a sense of failure, and they do not often treat the experience lightly. There is a lot of heartache and emotional suffering involved which can result in illness.

The divorced couple, their children, grandparents and other relatives can feel a sense of loss that is equivalent to bereavement. Divorced couples and those closest to them must in a sense redefine their life history in terms of a re-evaluation of the marriage and the former partner they once loved. There are several studies of the divorce experience, such as Nicky Hart's *When Marriage Ends* (1976), covering this aspect of redefinition and adaptation to divorce.

> *Do you agree that divorce has such profound impacts? Contact someone who has experienced divorce in their family and conduct a sensitive in-depth interview to explore whether the issues described were present for them.*

Changing roles of women

Throughout the twentieth century there have been significant changes in the role of women in society, some of which we have examined. One factor to note regarding divorce is that now the majority of petitions, over 75 per cent, are made by women, which is the reverse of the situation in the 1960s (see Table 9.3).

Table 9.3 Divorce[1]: women taking the lead

Petitions filed[2] (thousands)	1961	1971	1976	1981	1984	1985	1986	1987	1988	1989
England and Wales										
By husband	14	44	43	47	49	52	50	50	49	50
By wife	18	67	101	123	131	139	131	133	134	135
Total	32	111	145	170	180	191	180	183	183	185

Notes:
1 This table includes annulment throughout.
2 Estimates based on 100% of petitions at the Principal Registry together with a 2 month sample of county court petitions (March and September)

Source: Office of Population Censuses and Surveys, Lord Chancellors Department, General Register Office (Scotland)

> *Describe the trends indicated in this table.*

The figures seem to indicate that there is widespread dissatisfaction among women with their marriages and probably more specifically their husbands.

Explain this statement. It would be useful to refer back to the 'Domestic division of labour' section of Chapter 5.

This would support Jesse Bernard's view that in a relationship there are two marriages, one experienced by the husband and the other experienced by the wife. The perceptions associated with each can be different (Bernard 1976).

Explain why a husband and wife might have very different perceptions of their marriage.

It may be that many husbands regard their attitudes, involvement and approach to their marriage as satisfactory, but this is often not the way their wives feel about them. We have already noted one area where the discrepancy is obvious – the domestic division of labour (see pages 67-70). There is clear evidence of inequality in that wives do the majority of laborious and monotonous tasks such as cleaning, washing and ironing. Husbands may think this is reasonable, but many wives, particularly those who work outside the home, are likely to be dissatisfied, and this can be a source of the differing perceptions that husbands and wives have of their marriages.

The increase in women's employment (in 1994 over half the workforce was female) has created greater opportunities for women to be economically and financially independent than they enjoyed in the past. Until recently, many women who were unhappily married had to remain so and were trapped in 'empty shell' marriages because of their inability to support themselves and the lack of opportunity for divorce.

Explain the term 'empty shell' marriages.

Nevertheless it should be remembered that women's average earnings are still less than 75 per cent of men's. Many women are in low-paid and part-time work, so their opportunities for financial independence are not great.

Connected with women's growing independence are changing attitudes among growing numbers of women in Western societies towards marriage and family life. It appears that an increasing proportion of women do not see marriage as the only available option for fulfilling themselves in life, and look to other goals and achievements such as their careers and social activities such as sports and leisure.

If you are female, consider your own future. Do your ambitions reflect a wide range of available options? Discuss this issue with your fellow students, male and female.

Some recent support for this hypothesis comes from a survey that indicated that young women are starting to rate successful careers as more desirable than marriage and family life. However, the research was carried out with a small sample of students so it may not reflect the majority view.

1 Explain why this research may not be representative, using class differences as part of your answer.

2 Conduct a small survey among young women from a range of backgrounds. For instance, in a college you could interview students on A-Level,

Hairdressing, Catering and other courses. As a further comparison, extend the research to a group of young males, first asking them similar questions about their ambitions, and then questioning them about the ambitions they would expect from a future wife.

3 Prepare a report and present it to your class. If others have carried out similar research, it would be useful to compare results.

4 Such results could be used for a project on the theme of 'Gender differences in perceptions of marriage', for which you would conduct wider research along the above lines.

Privatization of the family

If the family has become a 'haven in a heartless world', as some sociologists have suggested, there is a cost: people in marriages have become reliant on fewer other people for support, and the emotional intensity within families can increase.

Geographical separation from the extended family can mean there is no one to talk to when marital difficulties arise; for example, it may be difficult for a wife to discuss problems with her mother, which often occurred in Bethnal Green, the working-class community studied by Young and Wilmott in the 1950s. Men are generally reluctant to go to marital guidance agencies such as Relate, so problems can worsen, resulting in eventual divorce.

1 What opportunities would men have had in the past to discuss their problems that are not available for them today? Think of social activities, and how husbands and fathers are now more home-centred in their time outside work.

2 Do men 'bottle up' their feelings more than women and, if so, why is this?

3 What outlets for their emotions do men have?

Demographic trends

An aspect of the privatization of the family has been a decline in average family size; a one- or two-child family has become the norm in late twentieth-century Britain. This adds to the emotional intensity of family life that we noted above, and echoes the arguments of the radical psychiatrists featured in Chapter 6.

It was once commonly held that large families were 'happier' than smaller families, but of course this often meant an increased workload for women, who may well not have been as 'happy' as their husbands. Such an oversimplification does not address possible differences in the quality of relationships between husbands and wives in families of different sizes. There is also a difficulty in operationalizing 'happiness' for research of this kind.

1 Explain the problem of operationalizing 'happiness', drawing on the methods sections of your textbooks.

2 Conduct a survey among fellow students regarding family size and 'happiness'. How would you define 'large' families? What difficulties are involved in such research?

Changed expectations of marriage

It has been suggested by sociologists and other commentators that perceptions and expectations within today's marriages are qualitatively different from those of the past.

Marriage used to be primarily an economic or financial arrangement in which women were dependent on men. For reasons examined elsewhere, this has changed somewhat, and today the emphasis in marriage is on equality and partnership as desirable qualities of the relationship between husbands and wives. As Bernard's concept of 'two marriages' indicates (see pages 126), there may be some differences between women and men with regard to this. It seems that women tend to value companionship and friendship with their partners more than men do.

Discuss in pairs whether this is true. Conduct a small survey on expectations of marriage to see if you can detect any gender differences.

There is today a considerable diversity of roles and expectations within marriage, and variations in the degree to which they are shared. For example, either or both partners may expect the other to be:

- a financial provider for dependants – today husbands and wives frequently share this role;

- a compatible sexual partner – increasingly emphasized in modern times;

- a parent in a child-centred environment – with fathers and mothers equally involved;

- a friend and confidant – someone to discuss problems with and provide emotional support;

- a homemaker – providing or helping to provide a comfortable, secure and safe environment and a good standard of living.

Fulfilling these and related roles can be demanding, particularly for the many people who face increased work pressures. The resultant stress and having to juggle with the different roles can cause marital tensions which sometimes lead to divorce.

Who divorces?

Divorce rates differ according to several sociological categories, notably:

- age,

- social class and occupation,

- ethnicity,

- religion,

- family experience of divorce, and

- status differences between partners.

Age

Generally speaking, the younger the age at marriage the higher the chances of eventual divorce. This is particularly noticeable among teenagers, for whom pregnancy is often a factor pushing them into marriage. Divorce rates for this age group are around 50 per cent.

The reasons for this very high rate of marital breakdown include family disapproval and rejection, financial insecurity, housing problems, immaturity and eventual 'drifting apart' as the couple get older.

1   Construct an imaginary case study of such a young couple, providing details of their circumstances that could lead to strains in their marriage.

2   Show how Durkheim's concept of 'social integration' from the Sociology of Suicide *(see your textbooks for this subject) can be applied to explain the marital instability of teenage couples.*

Social class and occupation

The middle classes tend to have lower divorce rates than the working class. The unemployed have the highest rate of all, regardless of former occupational status. The same applies to income levels and security of occupation, with lower-income groups and those of insecure occupational status showing high divorce rates. However, some middle-class and higher-income groups such as actors, authors, artists, company directors and hotel keepers do have high divorce rates.

Explain why you think these high-income groups have higher rates of divorce than others of their class.

The general picture is that economic well-being, job security and a good standard of living are associated with marital stability. Evidence to support this comes from couples who commonly cite financial difficulties as a cause of tensions within a marriage.

How might this observation be interpreted to lend support for arranged marriages (see pages 119–22)?

Ethnicity

Overall divorce rates are lower among ethnic minority groups, particularly those that adhere to cultural traditions centring around religious and related core values. Where arranged marriages are part of the culture the experience and foresight of parents and older family members are seen as beneficial, providing a sound basis for a stable and lifelong marriage and thus avoiding the high divorce rates associated with the tradition of choosing a marital partner on the basis of romantic love.

However, it can also be argued that divorce is a less available option for ethnic minorities because of the isolation and rejection by family and community that the couple would experience. In particular, a divorced woman would face ostracism and would have no available means of support. Thus it could be argued that 'empty shell marriages'(see page 126) are more likely to result when relationships break down, so the true picture of marital success is difficult to ascertain.

Discuss and evaluate the arguments offered above, and then answer these questions:

> *1 Are ethnic minority marriages happier than others because divorce rates are much lower?*
>
> *2 Is an arranged marriage a better basis for marriage than romantic love?*

Religion

In general, marriages in which the partners have committed religious beliefs have lower divorce rates than those with little or no such commitment, but as in the discussion of ethnicity the argument can be made that religious couples stay together for fear of possible ostracism from family and community and thus remain trapped in empty shell marriages.

Catholicism forbids divorce, and a divorcee cannot remarry in a Catholic Church. Other religions, while disapproving of divorce, may be more tolerant and in some denominations a divorcee can have a church wedding.

> *1 Research religious attitudes to divorce in your area. For instance, interview a priest or religious official and also examine the relevant issues among your fellow students, friends and neighbours.*
>
> *2 Consider how Durkheim's concept of 'social integration' can be applied to the incidence of divorce among ethnic and religious groups.*

Family experience of divorce

You are more likely to divorce if you have experienced the divorce of your parents or close family members. Several reasons have been offered for this, including the possibility that psychological insecurity and instability among children of divorced parents produces divorce-prone adults. Hart (1976) argues that within divorced families there may be greater acceptance of divorce as a solution to marital difficulties.

Contrary to this somewhat gloomy view, there is now some evidence from American research that in certain circumstances a child of divorced parents can develop a mature outlook upon their eventual adult relationships and may be determined not to repeat his or her parents' experience. The key factors here are the explanations the divorcing parents offer to the child and the degree to which the child is involved in coming to terms with the eventual divorce. The best outcome is where the child does not feel guilty or unloved by either parent. Children treated in this way can develop a sound awareness of the possible difficulties within marriage which gives them a good basis to choose a partner in adulthood.

> *Discuss in detail whether you agree that the experience of divorce can be a positive one for the children.*

Social and status differences between partners

Divorce rates are usually higher where couples are from different social backgrounds. The discrepancy can be in terms of:

- social class – as when the daughter of a doctor and a lecturer marries the son of a factory worker and a lorry driver;

- race – when, for instance, a black female marries a white male;

- ethnicity – as when a Muslim girl marries a Sikh boy;

- religion – e.g. a Catholic girl marries a Protestant boy; or

- age – as when a 60-year-old woman marries a 30-year-old man.

Statistically such differences are unusual: we have already noted that choice of partner is generally channelled along lines of similar social origins. Where such marriages do occur, the experience of ostracism and isolation from the wider community may once again play a part, but in this case it will tend to create instability in the relationship, particularly in areas where racial, ethnic or religious tensions are high or even the source of overt violence, as until recently in Northern Ireland. Cultural differences can also build an element of incompatibility into a relationship, as for example in the case of a husband from a patriarchal cultural background who has different expectations about domestic roles and responsibilities from his wife who has come from an egalitarian cultural background.

The children of such marriages can add further complexities. For example, issues of racial, religious or ethnic identity can be a source of confusion for the child. Racism can have especially painful consequences, since some mixed-race children may find it impossible to accept either black or white identity.

Despite these difficulties, or perhaps because of them, such marriages may gain strength from overcoming adversity, and hence produce happy and stable families.

As for occupational differences, where they exist it is usually the husband who enjoys the higher job status, which is not surprising given the gender inequalities that still exist in employment opportunities for men and women. However, the stereotyped tale of love bridging differences in social status often featured in romantic fiction, as when a male doctor marries a female nurse, is not commonly found in the real world. A doctor is more likely to marry another doctor or someone of equivalent professional status.

 Imagine that a female doctor marries a male nurse. Examine the possible difficulties faced by the husband in such a relationship. Compare this to the case of a male doctor marrying a female nurse. What does this tell you about the roles and expectations of men and women in society?

Consequences of divorce

Looking at the positive side, the increased availability and acceptance of divorce could be seen as enabling people to terminate unhappy relationships, leaving them free to seek a more settled personal life. However, in recent years more attention has been paid to the negative consequences of high divorce rates.

Political consequences

In Britain, Conservative politicians have raised the issue of the high economic costs to society of divorce in terms of the increase in welfare benefit payments to one-parent families. Most such families are headed by a woman and many suffer financial hardship and poverty, so they claim state benefits as their only available means of support.

A solution to the increasing drain on the Exchequer has been sought through making divorced fathers more financially liable for their children. This was the guiding principle behind the setting up of the Child Support Agency (CSA) in 1993. Since then there has been growing controversy, featuring newspaper headlines and media reports of suicides of divorced fathers, allegedly as a result of receiving greatly increased payment orders from the CSA for the upkeep of their children. A particular source of resentment has stemmed from the principle enshrined in the 1990 Children and Young Person's Act that the maintenance assessment for a child should also consider the person who cares for and looks after them, in most cases the mother. There have been many marches and public protests, mainly by the men concerned but in some cases supported by their new partners who resent indirectly having to contribute towards the support of former wives and children.

The New Right (see Chapter 8) disapproves of easy divorce and advocates a strengthening of marriage and family life for the sake of a healthier society. If marriages do break down every effort should be made through an agency such as the CSA to hold fathers responsible for the maintenance of their children and ex-wives so that the state and the taxpayer have to bear less of the financial burden.

For different reasons some feminists initially supported the principle behind the CSA, focusing on the poverty of former wives as compared to their ex-husbands who within a few years of divorce usually recover financially and in the longer term are no worse off than they were, and may even be more prosperous. Some Conservative politicians reinforced this view by claiming that the purpose of the CSA was to make sure errant fathers paid for the support of their children, thus alleviating the poverty of their former wives or partners.

Some men's groups, in particular Families Need Fathers, have been at the forefront of protest against the CSA, gaining a high media profile as a result. There have been recent newspaper accounts of former wives who have gained from the CSA and other accounts of the new partners of divorced husbands who have lost out.

Carry out library research of back issues of newspapers and journals (or use CD-ROM if available) to find out as much as possible about the CSA, and present a report explaining the issues involved.

Social consequences

The divorced couple have to go through a number of accommodations and adjustments to their new situation. Paul Bohannan (1970) explains the stages involved, referring to them as overlapping 'stations of divorce', as follows:

- Emotional divorce: within the deteriorating marriage tension and rows occur.

- Legal divorce: the grounds on which the marriage is ended, such as adultery or separation, are determined.

- Economic divorce: wealth and property are divided up.

- Co-parental divorce: issues of child custody (now access) and visiting rights are decided.

- Community divorce: alterations are made to friendships and other social relationships. Former friends may lose contact with one or more of the former partners because of divided loyalties.

- Psychic divorce: ties of emotional dependence are severed, and the former partners face up to the demands of living apart.

Explain each of the above 'stations' in more detail, giving appropriate examples.

Thus, despite increased acceptance and availability, divorce is still a difficult and painful experience for many couples. In the 1990s there have been attempts to deal with such problems through Family Mediation Services. There have been successful pilot schemes, but at the time of writing there are insufficient funds for such services and they are not widely available.

Find out more about Family Mediation Services and their work. The Citizens' Advice Bureau and libraries could be useful sources of information. Suggest ways to enable couples to cope with divorce more easily.

It's good to talk

We must think of the children – the sad refrain of divorcing parents is heard often, but children have very few legal rights when families split up. Will the proposed new divorce laws, which are due to go through Parliament this autumn, help to ensure that children's needs are put first?

The proposals include the much talked-about end to the 'quickie' divorce obtained by citing adultery or unreasonable behaviour. For couples seeking a non fault divorce based on separation with consent, although it is likely that there will be a minimum period 'for consideration and reflection' under the new rules. Mediation is to play a much bigger role in divorce settlements, to keep them out of the courts.

Most organizations concerned with children's welfare believe that abolishing the fault-based elements of divorce will mitigate bitterness and hostility, which can only be good for children. But there are worries that the new legislation could work against children's best interests in other ways.

The Children's Legal Centre argues that while a minimum 'cooling off' period such as 12 months can be useful for sorting out the best provision for children, it could be undesirable and even dangerous where one partner is violent, mentally ill or has drug or alcohol problems – they believe that abridgment of the period should be possible.

'There has to be will on both sides for mediation to work' says the

CLC's Nichola Wyld. 'Where there is domestic violence, for example, or if people can't agree, the court must intervene.' Mediation should be provided as a public-funded extra to legal services, not a money-saving replacement, Wyld argues.

A move away from the courts could also give children less right to have their views taken into consideration. If a divorce goes to court, a child's opinions will be sought by a Court Welfare Officer as required in the Children Act. But there is no such requirement for mediation.

Some mediation services are making efforts to include children in the process. National Family Mediation, with 60 centres around the UK, has been researching the way children are involved in mediation. 'We're introducing training for mediators to help parents consult their kids, or to consult the children directly where parents are unable to do it,' says their director Thelma Fisher. 'We're there to help with decision-making, we're not a counselling service.'

The NFM has no desire to see mediation made compulsory: 'some people are advised not to use it, and it should be voluntary. But mediation could be used more frequently than it is now – research shows that it helps parents to focus on the needs of the children,' says Fisher.

Children do have the right to challenge decisions made about custody and access in court, if they are judged to be of sufficient maturity and understanding. Some children have applied to force a separated parent to maintain contact against that parent's wishes, for example.

Parental separation is one of the main issues tackled by the Children's Legal Centre helpline (0171 359 6251, Monday to Friday, 2pm to 5pm), along with school discipline and bullying, taking children into care, and juvenile crime.

Guardian, 28 March 1995

Effects on children

It used to be thought by sociologists and others that children would not be harmed in the long term by the divorce of their parents. Distress and a sense of loss might be experienced in the short term, but by adulthood the child of divorced parents was expected to be no different from a child brought up in a stable marriage, thanks to a 'bounce back' effect.

Recently this view has been challenged by several studies in Britain and America which have examined the long-term effects of divorce and reached some worrying conclusions. In the 1980s, research by Bristol and Oxford universities and in the early 1990s a study in Exeter all came to similar conclusions about longer-term social problems for children associated with divorce. Such problems include:

- underachievement at school,

- unemployment and poverty,

- a heightened propensity to divorce as adults,

- higher than average levels of alcoholism and drug abuse,

- a higher likelihood of mental and physical illness and even of suffering fatal traffic accidents,

- increased criminal convictions, and

- a higher than average propensity to attempt or commit suicide.

'Feuding parents better for children than separation'

Research published today will be used to lend weight to the argument that feuding couple should try to stay together for the sake of the children.

A study of 152 children in Exeter found that those being brought up by both parents experience fewer health, school and social problems than those whose parents had split up.

Children of parents whose relationship was in difficulties, but were still together, fared worse than those whose parents' relationsip was good. But they fared much better than children hwose parents had parted.

The finding will fuel the debate over parental reponsibility and lone parenthood and will give valuable ammunition to the pro-family lobby, which has been relying on dated and contentious resarch.

The 152 Exeter children, aged 9–10 and 13–14, were selected from 620 families and were paired so that 76 came from intact, two-parent households and 76 from 're-ordered' families. Pairings were based on factors including age, mother's education, and their social class as measured by occupation.

Of the 76 children not living with both parents, 31 were in lone-parent households, 26 had become part of a stepfamily and 19 had experienced multiple family disruption through at least three different homes.

Researchers Monica Cockett and Dr John Tripp of Exeter Universityís department of child health, found marked differences. The children from re-ordered families were at least twice as likely to have problems of health, behaviour, school work and social life and to have a low opinion of themselves.

The re-ordered families as a whole were more likely to be living on social security, less likely to have a car and had typically moved house more often – factors which would probably have added to the strain on children.

However, Dr Tripp say the research shows clearly that the loss of a parent is the critical factor. Its importance overshadows other factors such as conflict between parents still living together.

'We know conflict is damaging in that it undermines children's well-being and makes them feel less good about themselves,' Dr Tripp says in tonight's edition of BBC1's Panorama.

'But our data suggests that is really a very minor effect compared to the effects that we see when a parent leaves home.'

The research, sponsored by the Joseph Rowntree Foundation, also found that only a third of the children had frequent, regular contact with a parent who had left the family home.

Children Living in Re-ordered Families – Social Policy Findings 45; JRF, The Homestead, 40 Water End, York, YO3 6LP; free.

Guardian, 7 February 1994

The studies compared children from similar backgrounds in respect of class, parental occupation, status, ethnicity and similar variables. The divorce of one's parents clearly emerges as a key variable in the likelihood of experiencing the social problems identified.

Such findings have led some sociologists to postulate a 'divorce inheritance' which is passed through the generations. However, William J. Goode (1956) offers a somewhat different perspective, suggesting that most of the problems exhibited by the children of divorced parents actually exist in many families well before the divorce occurs. For example, a boy who receives little attention and affection from his parents may be badly behaved and ill-disciplined, causing problems at school for several years while his parents are still married. If his behaviour continues after their divorce, it may be wrongly interpreted as a product of the divorce.

1 Consider the points made in the last few paragraphs as well as the more positive views about the effects of divorce, and assess the differing views offered. What can be done to alleviate the possible harmful effects of divorce?

2 Contact your local Social Services Children's Department to see if you can interview a social worker involved in such matters to find out what help may be provided for divorced families.

Current trends in divorce

In 1991, divorces in Britain reached their highest-ever level – 171,000, which was also the highest in Europe. Overall there has been a stabilization in annual numbers since the early 1980s, but this has to be offset by the declining numbers of marriages and the rising levels of cohabitation.

Remarriage rates (currently around one in three marriages is a remarriage) continue to be high among divorcees, but in recent years increasing numbers – particularly of divorced women – seem to be opting for cohabitation rather than remarriage in their new relationships.

Alternatives to the stereotypical nuclear family, such as one-parent families and reconstituted families (see Chapter 10), continue to rise in popularity. The numbers

Figure 9.6 Numbers of children in Great Britain with divorced parents

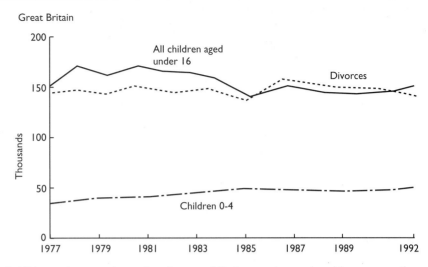

Great Britain

of children who experience the divorce of their parents are also rising – currently around one in five children undergo this experience.

A pattern of *serial monogamy* (monogamous marriages to a succession of partners) and, in admittedly a few cases, *serial divorce* (a divorce 'career') is developing. This trend is most prominent in the USA, where it is found that second marriages have higher divorce rates than first marriages, but the same is true in Britain and similar European countries.

> *Explain why divorce rates are higher the 'second time around'. (It might help to look back at the section on the CSA.) Can this explain why 'serial monogamy' and the divorce 'career' are growing phenomena?*

Explanations that sociologists have offered include:

- the 'instability' of the people concerned – a psychological explanation;
- the economic hardships faced when setting up new households;
- the stress of step-parenting in a society that places great emphasis on biological (sometimes called 'natural') parentage;
- tensions and complexities that continue from former marriages which could involve jealousy over a younger new partner, and children being used as 'pawns' in a game of emotional blackmail.

Conclusion

Current trends indicate that four out of ten contemporary marriages will eventually end in divorce, but of all marriages through all age groups the rate is around one divorce for every seven marriages. So there is still a strong case for arguing that the majority still marry 'until death us do part' rather than 'until divorce us do part'. Moreover, most children are raised by two married parents in a nuclear family household. Nevertheless, this does not minimize the impact of rising levels of divorce and the costs and suffering experienced by many people as a result.

Bibliography and further reading

Bernard, J. (1976) *The Future of Marriage*, Harmondsworth: Penguin

Bohannan, P. (1970) *Divorce and After*, New York: Doubleday

Coleman, D, and Salt, J. (1992) *The British Population*, Oxford: Oxford University Press

Giddens, A. (1993) *Sociology*, 2nd edn, Cambridge: Polity Press

Goode, W.J. (1956) *World Changes in Divorce Patterns*, New Haven, Connecticut: Yale University Press

— (1963) *World Revolution and Family Patterns*, New York: Free Press

Hart, N. (1976) *When Marriage Ends*, London: Tavistock

Höllinger, F. and Haller, M. (1990) 'Kinships and social networks in modern societies: a cross-cultural comparison among seven nations', *European Sociological Review*, Vol. 6

Essay questions

1 'The rise in cohabitation rates in Britain is a symptom of the increased instability of families and households.' Discuss.

2 Examine the effects upon society of the rise in divorce.

3 'Most people marry and remain so "until death us do part"'. What are the consequences for current debates about marriage and family life?

4 Four out of five contemporary marriages will end in divorce, yet five out of ten will reach their Silver Wedding Anniversary. Discuss the implications for the stability of marriage as an institution in modern Britain.

5 'You could say I lost my faith in science and progress,/You could say I lost my belief in the Holy Church . . . /But if I ever lose my faith in you/There'd be nothing left for me to do' (Sting, 'If I ever lose my faith in you'). In what way could these lyrics be seen as a retreat into the privatized world of relationships? How might sociologists link such an 'ideology' to the rising breakdown of marriage?

Coursework suggestions

A number of project ideas have been suggested throughout this chapter. Carry out detailed research into any of the trends examined, such as the impact of divorce on family members (including the extended family). This could be a case study activity, or you could conduct research into the history of divorce legislation. Alternatively, you could investigate the origins of the CSA and its current effects, or research the composition and activities of pressure groups opposed to the CSA.

Stimulus – response questions

Item A

Sociologists have clear evidence about some of the factors which contribute to the breakdown of a marriage. A marriage between two people from very different backgrounds is more at risk of divorce. The divorce rate is higher in urban than rural areas. Marriages after a very short acquaintance are also risky. But the most crucial factor could be age. One in two teenage brides, and six out of ten teenage bridegrooms can expect their marriage to end in divorce.

In 1982, 42,000 of the couples who were divorcing had no children. Nevertheless there were 158,000 children under the age of sixteen involved in parental divorce in 1982.

Item B

The rise in the divorce rate does not mean that people have lost faith in marriage as an institution. In 1982 about 64 per cent of all marriages were first marriages for both partners. In 19 per cent of marriages one partner was remarrying and in 16 per cent both partners were remarrying. Unfortunately, the divorcee who marries again is almost twice as likely to get divorced again!

Source: adapted from A. Wilson, *Family*, London: Routledge, 1985.

Item C

The marriage rate has fallen by more than a half since 1971, while the number of divorces is reaching new records, and one in 12 couples is cohabiting.

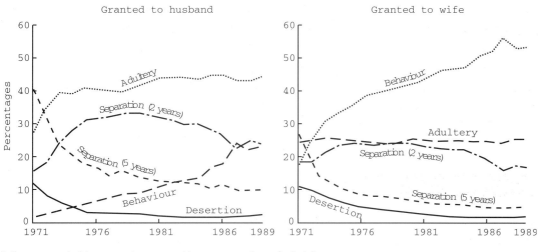

1 Decrees granted to one party on more than one ground are included in the 100 per cent base but have not been plotted.

Source: Lord Chancellor's Department

Divorce decrees granted by grounds

In the 12 months to September 1990, the rate of people marrying for the first time in England and Wales fell below 40 per 1000 people aged over 16. This compares with a rate of 82.3 in 1971 and 51.7 in 1981, while the rate of remarriage among divorcees has fallen even more steeply.

According to an analysis published by the Government's Office of Population, Censuses and

Surveys (OPCS), 34 per cent of divorced men and 22 per cent of divorced women are cohabiting.

The OPCS says the number of marriages is falling by about 4 per cent a year. The rate, which is falling more steeply and now stands at 39.6, is estimated to have dropped by 31 per cent for men and 26 per cent for women during the 1980s.

The remarriage rate among divorcees has

plummeted from 227.3 in 1971 to 129.5 in 1981 and 68.3 in the 12 months to September 1990.

In a study of cohabitation, the OPCS calculates that 1.2 million of a total of 13.9 million couples were living together outside marriage in 1989. Where the man was in his twenties, three in 10 couples were cohabiting; where he was in his thirties, the ration was one in 10.

On divorce, the OPCS reports that there were 153,000 decrees made absolute in 1990 and that there were almost 81,000, a record in the first 6 months of this year, a rise of 2.6 per cent.

It is estimated that while 6 per cent of marriages in 1974 ended in divorce within 5 years, the incidence rose to 10 per cent among 1984 marriages.

Source: adapted from an article in the *Guardian*, 6 April 1991.

Item D

As laws and procedures regulating divorce have altered, the divorce rate has tended to increase by leaps and bounds. Many people have suggested that the higher divorce rates reflect an underlying increase in marital instability. Some commentators have gone further, and argued that more permissive divorce laws in themselves cause marital breakdown.

Source: adapted from T. Bilton *et al., Introductory Sociology*, 2nd edn, London: Macmillan, 1987.

Item E

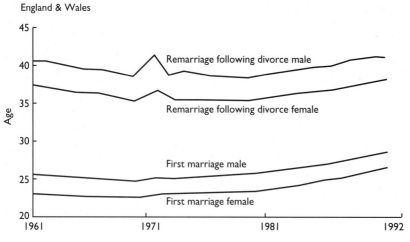

England & Wales

Source: Office of Population Censuses and Surveys

Marriage and remarriage: by sex

(a) According to the author of Item A, what could be the most crucial factor in leading to the breakdown of marriages? **(1 mark)**

(b) How do the grounds for divorces granted differ between husbands and wives (Item B)? **(4 marks)**

(c) Identify the percentage changes in the rate of marriage for men and for women in the 1980s (Item C) **(2 marks)**

(d) Using information from the Items above and elsewhere, assess the arguments for and against the view outlined in Item D that 'more permissive divorce laws in themselves cause marital breakdown' **(8 marks)**

(e) Using material from Item E and elsewhere, assess the view that the 'rise in the divorce rate does not mean people have lost faith in marriage as an institution' (Item A) **(10 marks)**

10 / *Contemporary trends*

Key ideas
- Single parent families/households
- Unmarried mothers
- Divorced mothers
- Life course/cycle
- The feminization of poverty
- Reconstituted (step) families
- Remarriage
- Step parents
- Step children

Key figures

- Warde & Abercrombie
- David Morgan
- Ellis Cashmore
- Burgoyne & Clarke
- Donna Smith

The subject of this chapter follows on from our discussion of the trends in marriage and divorce in Chapter 9. We shall be looking in detail at single-parent families or households and reconstituted families.

Single-parent families and households

Problems of definition

Close examination reveals that it is misleading to talk of *the* single-parent family; in fact there is a variety of circumstances in which single parenthood can occur. The word 'family' can mean quite different things according to the circumstances, and this has led some commentators to prefer the use of the term 'household', as we noted in Chapter 1.

 Do children have to live with two married parents to be judged to be living in a 'family'? Give reasons for your answer.

Figure 10.1
Lone parent
families in
Britain, 1991

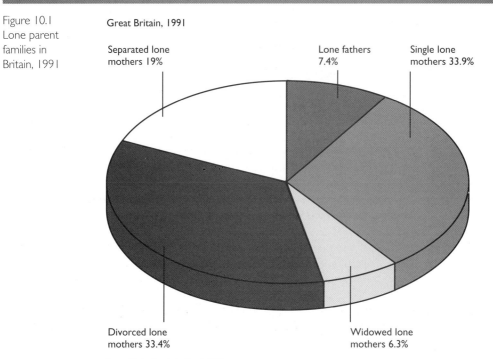

Great Britain, 1991

Separated lone
mothers 19%

Lone fathers
7.4%

Single lone
mothers 33.9%

Divorced lone
mothers 33.4%

Widowed lone
mothers 6.3%

Source: Haskey Population Trends, 1993

The following are the most common types of single-parent family:

- a young mother who has had an unplanned pregnancy that may be the result of a casual or unstable relationship (this type is often the subject of media disapproval, as in tabloid headlines such as 'The Scandal of Schoolgirl Mums');

Figure 10.2 An
abandoned mother and
child in Victorian times

- a widowed parent with children;

- a divorced parent with children;

- a formerly cohabiting parent with children;

- a woman who deliberately chooses to have a child outside marriage, cohabitation or a stable relationship with a partner.

Consider each of the above types of one-parent family, assessing the extent to which they meet with social approval or disapproval, and give reasons for the social judgement in each case.

For a full answer you can draw on the concepts of Labelling Theory and Stereotyping in the Sociology of Deviance.

You will have noticed that different levels of concern are expressed, depending on the type of single parenthood that is in question. Some single parents attract sympathy, for example widows and sometimes divorcées, particularly where a divorced wife has been wrongly treated by her husband. In earlier times single-parent families headed by a widow often won social approval, since according to the stereotype they were 'struggling against the odds' – a theme that lent itself well to heroic melodramas.

Today unmarried mothers – some of whom were accused in a controversial 1994 BBC TV *Panorama* programme of becoming pregnant in order to jump the waiting list for council housing – and women who have chosen to parent independently attract the most criticism. Unmarried mothers are also often perceived as representing a burden upon the taxpayer, and women who choose to bring up their children without husbands are felt to be a threat to the ideal of the stereotypical nuclear family.

In reality, single parenthood can reflect enormously different life opportunities and choices. Not all one-parent families are struggling to get by on state benefits or inadequate maintenance payments from a former partner: some are professional career women on high incomes who decide to have children without a stable relationship with a man, conceiving by means of artificial insemination or a 'surrogate' father.

However, the overwhelming evidence is that the majority of single-parent families experience significantly greater poverty and hardship than two-parent households. Recent figures show that around 17 per cent of lone parents work full time, and around 70 per cent experience poverty compared with around 20 per cent of two-parent families (*Labour Research* May 1992). The General Household Survey (1991) concluded:

> The differences in income between lone-parent families and other families are striking. In 1990, 53 per cent of lone parent families lived in households with a weekly income of £100 or less, compared with 4 per cent of married or cohabiting families.

Social trends

Statistics show a dramatic rise in the numbers of single-parent families. The General

Household Survey in 1991 indicated that one in five families with dependent children are now headed by a lone parent, which represents 1.3 million parents living with 2.1 million children.

The majority of single-parent families are headed by a mother: 18 per cent of all households are headed by a single mother, while 2 per cent of households are headed by a lone father. There is slow growth in the latter figure, but a more rapid rise in the former. One-third of all children will experience living in a single-parent family before they are sixteen.

Figure 10.3 Families headed by lone mothers and lone fathers as a percentage of all families with dependant children.

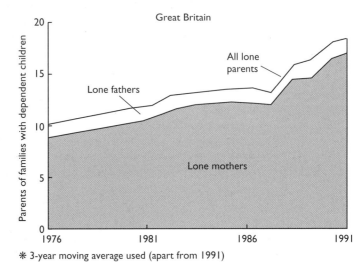

* 3-year moving average used (apart from 1991)

Source: Office of Population Censuses and Surveys

Britain has one of the highest proportions of single-parent households in the European Community. The majority of such households since the 1970s have come about as a result of divorce or separation. However, in a July 1992 report from the Family Policy Studies Centre, Jo Roll (cited in Denscombe 1993, p. 21) noted that in the late 1980s there was an increase in the numbers of younger unmarried women deciding to have children and living alone without their partners. As we saw in Chapter 8, the New Right – and in particular Charles Murray, with his concept of the 'underclass' – also focus their attention on fatherless families in working-class areas with high levels of unemployment. Such fathers are apparently deemed to be unnecessary as they cannot provide financial support and their parental involvement is otherwise low.

Explanations for the rise in single-parent families

The following points summarize some of the arguments discussed in previous sections in connection with divorce and raised levels of marital instability.

The first factor that is frequently cited is the rapid rise in divorce, particularly since the 1970s. Sixty per cent of single-parent households involve a divorced or separated partner.

Second, the demands placed on the partners in a marriage have changed. Today's emphasis on companionship and compatibility in a demanding and stressful world may be impossible to meet, so single parenthood becomes a preferred option.

Third, the role of women in particular has changed as they have become more independent. Women in unsatisfactory marriages feel less trapped than formerly because they have greater employment opportunities and thus financial independence from men.

Fourth, there has been a general increase in life expectancy. As people live longer, the number of years of marriage has increased compared to earlier times when the death of a spouse in early adulthood or middle age was a common experience. By the year 2000 the average life expectancy for females will be around eighty years and for males seventy-five years, meaning that a marriage may have a potential span of fifty years or more. This extension of married life may mean a higher probability of family breakdown among the middle-aged population, and with the increase of later parenthood may result in the formation of more single-parent households.

Fifth, families are on average smaller today than in former times. Thus the childrearing phase of their life cycle is now much shorter for many parents. If, as is traditionally assumed, children help to keep a family together, then childless families would be expected to be less stable than those with children. Furthermore, one-child families, or families with two children close in age, might not be as stable as larger families or families with two children further apart in age, where childrearing continues over a longer period. Taken together with the previous points about the increasing potential length of marriages and the companionship expectations which could become suffocating for the people concerned, it is easy to see that a sense of boredom, monotony and routine may set in without the distraction and demands that children can bring.

Figure 10.4 Keeping Mum and Dad together.

 Discuss the idea that children help to strengthen a marriage. Do you agree with the traditional assumptions as outlined above? Explain your answer, exchange experiences of large and small families among your class or peers.

Sixth, there has been change and variability in life circumstances. A traditional life cycle course can be represented as in Table 10.1 on page 146.

1 Consult an older person to see if a pattern such as the one depicted in Table 10.1 is applicable to them.

Table 10.1 A traditional life cycle

	Age	Life circumstances
Birth	0	Dependence on parents
Childhood	1–12	Dependence on parents
Adolescence	13–18	Dependence on parents
		Early work age for working class
Young adult	18–25	Work and courtship
Adult	25–45	Work, marriage, childrearing
Middle age	45–65	Work, children leave home
Old age	65+	Retirement, widowhood

2 *You could conduct research among a larger sample of different age groups to draw some life course comparisons and identify changes over a specified time period.*

The key feature of the sort of life cycle shown in the table is that, given some social class differences, it described the lives of most people fairly well. Today, however, there is much greater variability. Factors such as:

- rising levels of unemployment,

- prolonged education and the greater involvement of adults in higher education,

- increased numbers of graduates,

- flexible working patterns and a large increase in part-time work and job sharing,

- early retirement packages for middle-class professionals (for instance, teachers at fifty), and

- pressures at work, demands for increased productivity and high stress levels,

have all produced greater unpredictability during the lives of many people. Some sociologists now suggest that the term 'life cycle', with its connotation of a predictable succession of stages in the lives of most people, should be replaced with 'life course'. Warde and Abercrombie (1994) list the following additional factors that have disrupted previously established patterns:

- childbearing outside marriage,

- divorcees beginning second families,

- the public emergence of alternatives to heterosexuality,

- changing definitions of women's social role, and

- the tendency for people to live longer.

In particular connection with the growth of one-parent families we can add the following factors:

- There is now considerable variability in women's work patterns, which can veer between full-time and part-time work and may involve a variety of occupations.

- Higher education opportunities have expanded greatly for adult and mature students, notably women. This has produced what has been called the '*Educating Rita* syndrome', where unqualified working-class women gain qualifications and enter professions such as teaching, and in the process drift apart from their husbands.

- There has been an extension of the period of dependency until the mid to late twenties or longer as employment prospects diminish and the opportunities for young adults to set up their own homes and live independent lives have diminished. The result can be overcrowding in households and associated tensions and strains that can affect marriages and families.

*1 What sort of marital difficulties can arise from the '*Educating Rita *syndrome'?*

2 Consider a household with a married couple and their three children, one aged 24 and unemployed, one a student aged 22, and a 15 year old still at school. Discuss in pairs or small groups the interactions you would expect to encounter in such a household. Think in particular of the possible tensions, power struggles and related family dynamics. If appropriate this activity can be developed into a full role-play exercise and follow-up class discussion.

A seventh factor causing the increase in single parenthood has been a rise in the numbers of unmarried mothers associated with increased sexual activity among young people. Many young women, faced with hardship, poor employment prospects and an uncertain future, may have developed a 'devil may care' attitude to pregnancy even though birth control is available to them. Such mothers may set up single-parent households, or they may live at home with their parents. There has also been an

Figure 10.5 *Educating Rita*

Table 10.2 Current use of contraception * in Britain, by age, 1991

Current use of contraception* in Britain, by age, 1991				
	16–19	20–34	35–49	All aged 16–49
	(%)	(%)	(%)	(%)
Non-surgical				
Pill	31	37	6	23
IUD	0	5	6	5
Male condom	12	17	15	16
Cap	0	1	2	1
Withdrawal	1	3	3	3
Safe period	–	1	1	1
Spermicides	0	–	–	–
Injection	–	1	–	1
Surgical				
Female sterilization	0	5	22	12
Male sterilization	0	6	23	13
Total using at least one method	39	71	76	70

* By women aged 16 to 49

Source: General Household Survey

increase in the numbers of older middle-class women who have chosen single motherhood, as noted on page 143. Conversely, widowhood has become less important than it was as a cause of single parenthood: in 1971 widowhood accounted for 21 per cent of all lone mothers, but by 1991 this figure had dropped to 6.3 per cent.

Table 10.3 Teenage conceptions in England and Wales, by age, *

England and Wales			
		Rates	
	1981	1990	1991
Under 14	1.1	1.3	1.3
14	4.6	6.6	6.6
15	15.8	21.6	19.9
16	37.7	46.4	43.4
17	56.8	69.5	65.5
18	76.2	89.2	84.9
19	94.0	99.5	96.0
All aged under 20	57.1	69.0	65.3

*Conceptions per 1,000 women

Source: Office of Population Consenses and Surveys

Eighth, in recent times single-parent role models have frequently been featured in the mass media, indicating an increased acceptability of single parenthood. There is less emphasis on illegitimacy and less stigma associated with terms such as 'lone-parent household' and 'single-parent family' than there was to the label 'unmarried mother'.

Explain why the former terms are more 'neutral' than the latter.

Finally, relationship bonds between parents may be weaker than they were as a result of the increase in the incidence of cohabitation rather than marriage.

 Do you think that cohabitation represents a weaker bond between parents than marriage? Give your reasons.

Consequences of the increase in single-parent families

As we noted on page 105, the statistics clearly show the disadvantaged position of single-parent families. Of the three main sources that single parents can draw upon for economic support – former partners, the state and employment – the greatest provider is the state. The government has tried to redress this imbalance through the Child Support Agency (see page 132), but in fact the levels of support in terms of child benefits and childcare provision offered by the state in Britain are already among the lowest in Europe.

In Chapter 8 we considered New Right and related opinions on the effects single parenthood has on children; they focus on the low educational achievement, rates of criminality, poor health and similar social problems that can be detected among children in one-parent families. It is as yet an unresolved issue whether the causal factors are predominantly:

- *internal* to the household (for example, the absence of a father as a socialization and disciplinary agent and role model for male offspring), or

- *external,* arising from general problems associated with poverty and deprivation regardless of whether the child is raised by one or two parents.

Figure 10.6 Publicly funded child care in Europe

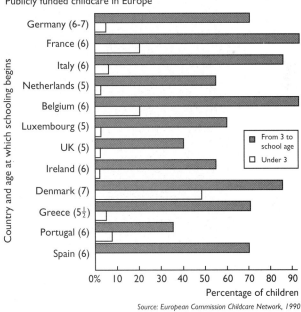

Publicly funded childcare in Europe

Source: European Commission Childcare Network, 1990

An illustration of the difficulty of separating such issues can be seen in education, where teachers' low expectations and stereotyping of single-parent family children can result in underachievement – an outcome described by Labelling Theory as a self-fulfilling prophecy.

> *Look this up in your textbook and write down the processes involved when teachers behave as just described.*

David Morgan (1994) concludes: 'The most cautious verdict would be that while it would be seen to be the case that children brought up in two parent households do tend to fare better than those who are brought up in single parent households, we still do not know enough about what causes these differences.'

Conclusion

Many concerns have been expressed about the rising numbers of single-parent families. Some see this phenomenon as a threat to the stability of normal family life, but in some cultures – for example, in Afro-Caribbean communities – single parenthood is more acceptable. Some stress the positive aspects of single parenting for women who are exploited, abused or poorly treated by men. Some see the single-parent household as a welcome sign of increased tolerance, diversity and choice in how people live their lives in modern societies.

Clampdown on single mothers to go ahead

The Government is to press ahead with plans to prevent single mothers from qualifying automatically for council houses, despite the current furore over the Prime Minister's back-to-basics strategy.

Sir George Young, the Housing Minister, will announce tomorrow that homeless single mothers will no longer be given priority for housing. It is a move that underlines Mr Major's determination that his strategy will not be derailed by the latest string of political scandals.

Sir George's statement in the Commons will inevitably fan the flames of the dispute over family values and will be seized on by the Labour Party as a blatant attack on single mothers.

Observer, 2 January 1994

Cashmore (1985) stressed the positive aspects by emphasizing that many single-parent families cope very well; they bring up their children on minimum resources in a stable, loving atmosphere with support from the neighbourhood and wider community – a picture that is at odds with the irresponsible, feckless image of single-parent families often portrayed in the media.

> *Examine the arguments for and against single-parent families and their role in modern societies.*

Reconstituted (step- or reordered) families

Another consequence of high divorce and remarriage rates is the increased proportion of households where one or both partners have been married before.

The stereotypical case of two divorced parents remarrying and bringing their children into a complex larger 'step' household is statistically rare, though it does occur.

 Describe the 'complexities' involved in such a 'step' household in terms of the relationships and interactions between family members.

This type of reconstituted family is unusual because children generally do not live with their fathers after divorce: over 80 per cent of children remain with their mothers.

 Why is this the case? Are fathers treated unfairly after divorce, as the pressure group Families Need Fathers suggests? What gender issues from the wider society does this illustrate?

Variations in reconstituted families

There are complexities in such households centring around the relationship between step-parent and step-child, as well as between step-brothers and step-sisters. Rivalries and tensions can develop.

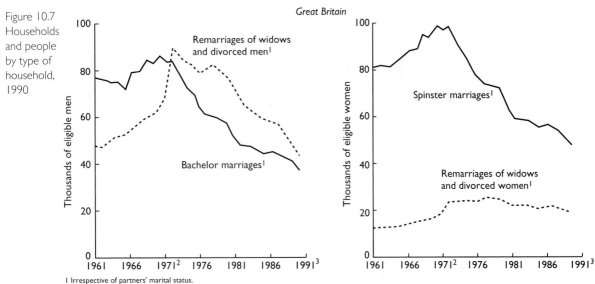

Figure 10.7 Households and people by type of household, 1990

1 Irrespective of partners' marital status.
2 The Divorce Reform Act 1969 came into effect in England and Wales on 1 January 1971.
3 1993 data for Scotland has been used for 1991.

Source: Office of Population Censuses and Surveys

Construct role-play exercises around the following case studies.

Case 1: A 45-year-old father of two teenage children has an affair with a 24-year-old divorcée with two small children. He divorces and remarries. His 42-year-old wife now lives as a single parent.

Case 2: Two divorcees remarry and set up a step-household with both sets of adolescent children. After a year they have a baby.

Explore the issues raised in terms of accommodations and tensions in both cases, assigning roles for all the people involved in the present and former relationships.

Evaluate the stability of reconstituted families in the light of these role-plays, giving your reasons. Then do some research in the library to find evidence in support of your points.

As with single-parent families, we can identify a variety of reconstituted family types. Burgoyne and Clarke (1982) differentiate three in terms of the life cycle:

- remarriages where the couple are able to and choose to have a child or children of their own within the step-family;

- remarriages where the couple choose to have no more children;

- older remarrying parents whose age prevents them from having children.

When we consider children from former marriages, the typology becomes more complex:

- In some reconstituted families the wife brings children from the former relationship but the husband does not; as we have noted, this is usually because in the main children opt to live with their mother. These children may feel divided loyalties if the 'new' father has children of his own, particularly when access visits are involved. If he has no children he has to adapt to fatherhood. If he is significantly younger than his wife and closer in age to her older children, then he may find it especially difficult to take on a paternal role, and the children may be particularly unwilling to accept him in that role.

- In a few reconstituted families the husband brings children from a former marriage whereas his 'new' wife has no children. Again, if she is significantly younger than he is, the 'new' wife may find it difficult to be a 'mother' to older children.

- There are also reconstituted families to which both partners bring children from former marriages. As we have already noted, there can be in-built tensions for all concerned, including stepbrother/stepsister rivalries.

Examine in turn each of these three arrangements, and summarize your views on the stability of the reconstituted family.

The complexity of the 'step' relationship

Western cultures with a strong ideological commitment to the nuclear family as the norm also emphasize the biological relationship between parent and child, as epitomized in the term 'natural' parent. Compared to a number of other cultures, much stress is placed on physical resemblance between parents and children ('Isn't he just like his Dad!'), a fact that has been linked historically to the importance of establishing paternity in patrilineal societies (see page 46).

In other societies, particularly tribal ones in which there is communal ownership of property, less emphasis is placed on the biological parent, especially the father. There may be a linguistic distinction between a *biological* and a *social* parent, with the latter being seen as the more important figure. A social father, for instance, could be a maternal uncle who is responsible for the child's upbringing and becomes a key father figure and role model.

The emphasis on physical, personality and character resemblance in Western societies creates in-built difficulties for the step-parent and step-child relationship.

> *Explore this problem by writing a dialogue between step-parent and step-child or a conversation between a step-father and a close friend discussing his new reconstituted family. You could then use this script in a role-play in front of the rest of your class.*

Donna Smith (1990) highlights some of the issues in an interview with a step-mother whose relationship had broken down:

> There's a lot of guilt. You cannot do what you would normally do with your own child, so you feel guilty, but if you do have a normal reaction and get angry you feel guilty about that, too. You are always so afraid you will be unfair. Her [the stepdaughter's] father and I did not agree and he would say I nagged if I disciplined her. The more he did nothing to structure her, the more I seemed to nag . . . I wanted to provide something for her, to be an element of her life which was missing, but perhaps I am not flexible enough.

> *1 Describe any differences that you might expect to hear in a similar account if a step-father were talking.*
>
> *2 Consider the word 'nagged'. How does this reflect negatively on women? Can the word be used in exactly the same way to describe a man who does the same? What do your answers tell you about gender differences in step-parenting?*

The step-parent, more likely a step-father, may feel jealous and resentful because the child provides visible evidence of his wife's former emotional and sexual relationship. Depressingly, the statistics on abused children show that a high proportion are abused by their step-fathers.

> *1 Nursery rhymes, folk legends and fairy stories – for instance, Snow White and the Seven Dwarfs – often portray a wicked step-mother, when the statistics on child abuse might lead one to expect more stories about the wicked step-father. Explain the discrepancy.*
>
> *2 Look through the library to find a variety of representations of step-parents in newspapers, magazines and children's books. Does a stereotypical picture emerge? If so, summarize what it is. This could be developed into a project on step-parenting in which you conduct research to explore some of the issues raised in this section.*

In the light of some of the tensions and difficulties outlined above it is perhaps not surprising that reconstituted families tend to be relatively unstable. There are higher divorce rates for second marriages than first marriages. However, the actual numbers of reconstituted families are relatively small, so generalization may be difficult.

It must also be noted that the focus in this chapter has been predominantly on the internal dynamics of such families. Strain could also be due to external factors such as economic hardship resulting from the obligation to support children from first marriages and the expense of running a large household with stepchildren. However, for divorced women remarriage may be a way of escaping the poverty of the single-parent household, as generally households involving remarriage have higher average incomes.

Despite its potential for instability, the reconstituted family is growing as divorce rates increase. Burgoyne and Clark (1982) estimate that 7 per cent of all children under 17 live with a step-parent. Moreover, recent trends suggest that as cohabitation grows and gains increasing acceptability the reconstituted family may more frequently centre upon a cohabiting couple.

Conclusion

This chapter has featured two 'newer' family structures that have attracted attention in connection with rising rates of divorce and marital breakdown in modern societies. However, it should be noted that in the past many families and households contained a diversity of relationships that were not always based on biological relationships between parents and children in a nuclear family. According to the accounts provided by historians (see Chapter 2), households commonly included step-relations, adopted orphans, spinster aunts and uncles, lodgers and others. Such complexities would probably make the modern reconstituted family seem relatively stable.

Bibliography and further reading

Burgoyne, J. and Clark, D. (1982) 'Reconstituted families', in R.N. Rapoport, M.P. Fogarty and R. Rapoport (eds) *Families in Britain*, London: Routledge

Cashmore, E. (1985) 'Rewriting the script', *New Society*, December

Denscombe, M. (1993) *Sociology Update*, Leicester: Olympus

Morgan, D.H.J. (1994) 'The family', in *Developments in Sociology*, Vol. 10, Ormskirk: Causeway

Smith, D. (1990) *Stepmothering*, London: Harvester

Warde, A. and Abercrombie, N. (1994) *Family, Household and the Life-Course*, Lancaster: Framework Press

Essay questions

1 Examine the sociological issues and debates surrounding the growth of the single parent family in contemporary Britain.

2 'The reconstituted or step family involves a complex pattern of relationships which could be seen as a basis for instability.' Examine this view in the context of a rise in the numbers of such households.

Coursework suggestions

Examine the issues surrounding single parent and/or reconstituted families. This would involve the use of household statistics from sources such as Social Trends. You will need to think carefully about research on such a private matter. Do you have friends or relations with whom you could conduct sensitive, in-depth qualitative interviews? What about an investigation of issues surrounding childcare and its effects on employment opportunities of single parent households?

Reconstituted families would need similar sensitivities regarding your research, for example it may be inadvisable to look at step parenting unless you know the people concerned very well.

Stimulus – response questions

Item A

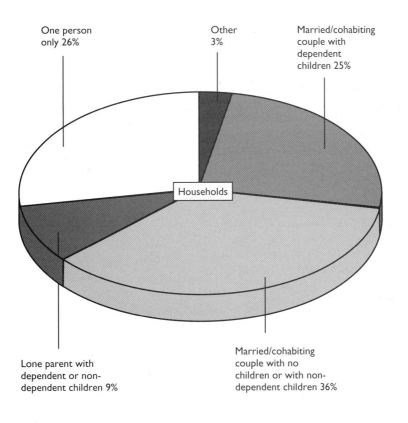

One person only 26%

Other 3%

Married/cohabiting couple with dependent children 25%

Households

Lone parent with dependent or non-dependent children 9%

Married/cohabiting couple with no children or with non-dependent children 36%

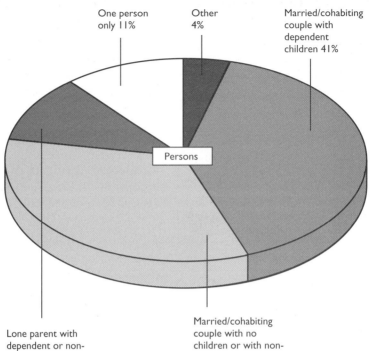

One person
only 11%

Other
4%

Married/cohabiting
couple with
dependent
children 41%

Persons

Lone parent with
dependent or non-
dependent children10%

Married/cohabiting
couple with no
children or with non-
dependent children 34%

Households and people by type of household, 1990

Source: General Household Survey 1990

Item B

Most adults still marry and have children. Most children are reared by their natural parents. Most people live in a household headed by a married couple. Most marriages continue until parted by death. No great change currently seems in prospect.

As headlines, such facts are the equivalent of an earthquake in Chile with nobody killed. They seem a far cry from current preoccupations about the family. Attention has focused on the rise in divorce, cohabitation, and one-parent families, and the fall in marriage and birth rates.

Of course some changes have occurred in marriage and family patterns. Their importance cannot be ignored. But they must be seen in the context of major continuities in family life.

The point is that snapshots of household types are misleading about families and they ignore the life-cycle. Even with universal marriage and parenthood, and no divorce or early death, there would always be many non-nuclear family

households, because the parents-plus-children unit is in a developmental phase. But it is one that is normal and is still experienced by the great majority of people.

Source: adapted from R. Chester, 'The rise of the neo-conventional family', *New Society*, 9 May 1985.

Item C

The possibility that the single-parent family is a distinct and viable family type requires discussion if for no other reason than that in 1990, one in six families in Britain was headed by a single parent, over ninety per cent of whom were women. Any adequate sociological discussion of this issue should not be influenced by the social stigma which still attach to single parenthood. What it is intended to do is explore whether the single-parent family, and the Afro-Caribbean single-parent family in particular, can be regarded as an alternative to the nuclear family and as an exception to its universality. The answer seems to be a qualified 'yes' to both these questions. In no modern society has the single-parent family replaced the nuclear family as the dominant family form but it is becoming increasingly common.

The number of lesbian and homosexual couples who bring up children is small but increasing. Such cases are unlikely ever to be more than a small minority of those concerning 'the family' but they are common enough to require placing within 'the sociology of the family'.

Indeed are such social units 'families'? They do not fulfil Murdoch's definition because they do not include 'adults of both sexes' and it is debatable whether the sexual relationships within them are 'socially approved'. As with the case of single-parent families, a more limited definition of the family is required if lesbian and homosexual families can, in fact, be defined as families.

It is historic fact that in almost every society the nuclear family has been the basic social unit. However, it is not quite true that the nuclear family is universal to all societies. The main exception is the single-parent family.

This does not mean that the nuclear family is breaking up, or, to use David Cooper's more dramatic word, 'dying'. Although the nuclear family survives and often flourishes still as the dominant family form, it is within the context of an increasingly pluralistic or varied pattern of family life.

The above changes can give little comfort to those who favour the extended family type structure. The modern family is typically small and second families especially so. No satisfactory general alternative to the nuclear family seems to exist.

Source: adapted from M. O'Donnell, *A New Introduction to Sociology*, 3rd edn, Walton-on-Thames: Nelson, 1992

Item D

Most societies have a prevailing image of what desirable family life would be like; modern Britain is no exception. In our every-day lives we are constantly subjected to such images. The process of socialization involves forming ideas of family life in children by a variety of devices including the stories that children read. In the old card game 'Happy Families', every family is made up of a

father, mother and two children. In adult life similar images are formed.

What does the image of the typical, normal or conventional family consist of? There are two parents aged between twenty and forty-five, legally married to each other, and not having been married to anyone else previously. Two children, born of these parents (and not others), live with them. The husband is in full-time employment while the wife is not. The wife takes on the bulk of the household tasks while the husband may help occasionally. The family is a self-contained, almost private, institution – a world to itself. Lastly, its members are happy.

It is doubtful if the image of the conventional family ever accurately described the majority of families in Britain.

Source: adapted from N. Abercrombie and A. Warde *et al.*, *Contemporary British Society*, Cambridge: Polity Press, 1988.

Item E

It is now a commonplace that the family is changing. There's more cohabitation, and more divorce. There are more single-parent families. More women work and more men stay at home. The family – the conventional couple with two kids idealized by advertisers and moral conservatives – is on its last legs.

But if this is the way things are moving why does everyone still bang on about the family?

This year's *British Social Attitudes* survey provides the crucial clue to the answer. For, this year, the survey asked a set of detailed questions on public attitudes to the family. The clear conclusion according to Sheena Ashford of Leicester University, author of this chapter in the survey's report, is that 'in their attitudes towards marriage and other family matters, the British emerge as highly and consistently conventional. The family may be dead but the idea of the family survives unchallenged.'

Views on women and work are not very radical either. The survey asked people what working arrangements they thought parents should have. For parents of under fives 76 per cent wanted father to be in full-time work with mother at home.

For parents with children in their early teens, only 19 per cent still insisted that mother should be at home. But still fewer – 17 per cent – favour equality (where both parents work either full or part time) between the parents. A full 60 per cent opt for the father to work full time and the wife part time.

Source: adapted from 'What the British are really thinking', in *New Society*, 30 October 1987

(a) According to Item A, what percentage of people lived as part of a married or cohabiting couple in 1988? **(1 mark)**

(b) Explain in your own words the meaning of the term 'life cycle' used in Item B (lines 18–19). **(2 marks)**

(c) The author of Item C argues that 'no satisfactory general alternative to the nuclear family seems to exist' (last two lines). Assess the extent to which this view is supported by sociological evidence. **(8 marks)**

(d) Explain what is meant by the 'image of the conventional family' (Item D, lines 12–13). **(3 marks)**

(e) Using material from the items above and elsewhere, assess the argument put forward in Item E that 'The family – the conventional couple with two kids idealized by advertisers and moral conservatives – is on its last legs' (Item E, lines 5–7). **(11 marks)**

11 The future of families and households

Key ideas
- Variability and diversity of families and households
- Stability of marriages and households
- Neo-conventional family
- Birth rates and demographic trends
- Average life expectancy
- Neo-extended families
- Grandparenthood
- Polygamy
- Communes
- Group marriages
- Kibbutz
- Older motherhood
- Reproductive technologies

Key figures

- Robert Chester
- Sandra Wallman

Despite some of the trends highlighted in previous chapters, the majority of people in the UK still eventually marry and have children. In 1988, 90 per cent of the population would either be married or expect to be married at some stage in their lives, and marriage is still the usual manner in which adults of the opposite sex live together. Most children are still brought up by two married biological parents. These children in their turn will probably marry and have children themselves, notwithstanding the increased variability in the life course (see Figure 9.3, page 118). The nuclear family household remains the predominant form in which parents and children live.

The Family Policy Studies Centre projects that, even by the year 2000, 75 per cent of the population of Britain will be married and 98 per cent of children will be brought up by their biological mother and around 75 per cent of children will live with both parents until adulthood.

This general background must be borne in mind when evaluating the numerous arguments, debates and issues surrounding the diversity and variability of families and households examined throughout this book. Statistics on household composition support the 'dominant nuclear family' model to a certain extent. Nevertheless there are different ways in which the statistics can be interpreted. Moreover, the controversy deepens when we consider the complex issue of whether the nuclear family is chosen freely as the expression of a desire for a fulfilling personal life, or whether people acquiesce in the arrangement because socialization and ideological conditioning have led them to believe that they have no alternative.

What the statistics show – two views

Table 11.1 People in British households, by type of household and family in which they live

	1961	1971	1981	1991	1992
Living alone	3.9	6.3	8.0	10.7	11.1
Married couple, no children	17.8	19.3	19.5	23.0	23.4
Married couple with dependent children[1]	52.2	51.7	47.4	41.1	39.9
Married couple with non-dependent children only	11.6	10.0	10.3	10.8	10.9
Lone parent with dependent children[1]	2.5	3.5	5.8	10.0	10.1
Other households	12.0	9.2	9.0	4.3	4.6
All people in private households (=100%)(thousands)	49,545	52,347	52,760	54,056	–

1 These family types may also include non-dependent children

Source: Office of Population Censuses and Surveys; General Register Office (Scotland): 1961, 1971, 1981 and 1991 Census data; 1992 General Household Survey

1   *What percentage change in one-person households occurred between 1961 and 1991? Give reasons for this change.*

2   *What proportion of people lived alone in 1992?*

3   *Explain the difference concerning people living alone between the percentages in Tables 11.1 and 11.2.*

4   *What percentage of people lived in a form of nuclear family in 1992?*

5   *If you wanted to highlight (i) the diversity of families and households, or (ii) the dominance of the nuclear family, which table would better support your argument and why?*

Most sociologists tend to support the diversity argument, that is, they hold the view that today's families and households exhibit a variety of types and options and that no one particular type of family or household is to be deemed better or more natural than any other. This may be because such sociologists reflect liberal-democratic or pluralist values that favour open-mindedness and tolerance of a wide range of lifestyles. So once again, as when issues surrounding New Right and other approaches were addressed, it should be recognized that the family has political and moral dimensions.

Robert Chester (1985) disagrees with the diversity approach to families and households. He uses household composition statistics to support the idea of a dominant nuclear family structure, echoing what we have said about how the majority of the population marry and have children. Chester would focus on Table 11.2, which refers to the numbers of *people* in households. He points out that such

Table 11.2 Households in Britain, by number of people in household				
	1961	*1971*	*1981*	*1991*
Household size				
1 person	14	18	22	27
2 people	30	32	32	34
3 people	23	19	17	16
4 people	181	17	18	16
5 people	9	8	7	5
6 or more people	7	6	4	2
Number of households (=100%)(millions)	16.2	18.2	19.5	21.9
Average household size (number of people)	3.1	2.9	2.7	2.5

Source: Office of Population Censuses and Surveys; General Register Office (Scotland); General Register Office (Northern Ireland)

tables can only provide a 'snapshot' at a particular time and do not capture the changes and dynamics that occur through people's life courses, which can be seen as 'moving pictures' spanning the range of experience from birth to death.

> *Write a brief life history of an imaginary 82-year-old woman to illustrate the changes of household circumstances that she has experienced.*

According to Chester, what is needed is a *past* and *future* as well as a *present* perspective on a person, a family or a household.

Figure 11.1 The family snapshot and the moving picture

1 *Taking the case of a typical single-parent family (as it is now), what will its household type probably have been in the past? According to overall trends, what may happen in the future? Do your answers support Chester's argument?*

2 *Take each of the other categories of household in Table 11.2 and follow a similar line of reasoning.*

Chester does recognize that modifications to the stereotypical nuclear family have occurred – there are now more working wives, and there is more symmetricality and democracy in relationships – and he uses the term 'neo-conventional family' in recognition of this. He concludes, however:

> Most adults still marry and have children. Most children are reared by their natural parents. Most people live in a household headed by a married couple. Most marriages continue until parted by death. No great change seems currently in prospect.

1 *Which four of the sentences just quoted from Chester have statistical support and could be regarded as factual? Which sentence is more contentious? Give reasons for your answers, drawing upon your work with previous chapters.*

2 *In groups or individually, gather statistics from the library to evaluate Chester's statement further.*

Demographic factors

Average family size in many modern societies has stabilized at around 1–2 children per family. Thus in some it has actually fallen below the replacement level of 2.1 children per family.

What is meant by 'replacement level'?

For instance Italy, with an average family size of 1.8, has a declining population. However, the position is very different in many Third World societies, where a larger average family size reflects higher infant mortality rates, a younger population and labour-intensive subsistence economies where the work of children is a vital source of family support.

In most European countries, including Britain, average life expectancy has increased. By the year 2000 it is expected to be 80 years for women and 75 years for men.

1 *Look up average life expectancy at the beginning of the twentieth century, then find out from textbooks and other sources what explanations have been offered for the increase. Make a set of notes on this topic.*

2 *Respond to the man in this cartoon. Conduct some research through textbooks and library sources to produce more rational explanations for the difference in life expectancy.*

Figure 11.2 A life-saving option?

Birth rates have fallen throughout the century, so the balance of the age structure of the British population has shifted and there are now larger proportions of old people compared to young people and children. This trend will continue into the next century.

 Examine some of the implications for families in the future of this shift in the age structure. Brainstorm in pairs and then report your ideas to the class, or write them up individually.

The older age group

On average, people now have living grandparents for a greater proportion of their lives than they used to. But there is a complicating factor in that there is a trend towards later marriage and childrearing, which is partly a reflection of the expansion and extension of educational opportunities to a later age and of the increased numbers of working women who give their careers and occupations high priority.

There has been publicity about a number of entertainers and media figures such as Anna Ford, the newscaster, and Diana Rigg, the actress, who have had first children in their late thirties and early forties. The average age of bearing a first child is creeping upwards to the late twenties, and is around thirty in the middle classes. Similar trends are emerging with male parenthood.

Explain why the age of bearing a first child is higher in the middle classes than the working classes.

The implications of this trend is that the younger grandparent, aged in the late thirties or early forties (stereotyped in 'Glamorous Grandmother' competitions in holiday resorts), who married at seventeen and had a daughter or son who also married at a

Figure 11.3 A four-generation family

similar age, will become more of a rarity. In the near future, grandparenthood could commonly begin in the early sixties. Since members of the present older generation are on average fitter and healthier and will consequently live longer than their parents, 'later' grandparenting may be less of a problem.

> *Follow through such trends and make predictions about greatgrandparenthood in the future.*

Social policy 'problems' of increased life expectancy

The growing numbers of retired and elderly people have been identified in recent years as a 'problem', particularly in areas such as health care and welfare benefits. The Thatcherite policies of the 1980s' Conservative government, with its emphasis on cuts in public expenditure, highlighted the issue with the closure of state and local authority funded homes for the elderly. These were replaced by private provision and a shifting focus on the responsibility of the family to support its members. This may at first seem laudable, but it is usually impractical to share such responsibility among family members. Given the large proportion of younger women who are in paid work the question arises as to who must sacrifice their jobs to take responsibility for the care of the elderly. The demands of childrearing are also difficult to balance with the time and energy involved in caring for an elderly and infirm person.

> *Why is it often assumed that the care of the elderly is the responsibility of a younger female relative? What changes in society would be required to distribute such responsibilities equally between men and women?*

Estate agents are increasingly advertising houses with areas deemed as 'suitable for conversion to a granny flat', which may reflect an increase in the numbers of elderly people living with younger kin – a sort of 'neo-extended family'.

> *Why a 'granny' flat? Look at past demographic statistics if you are unsure about your answer.*

It should be remembered that with longer life expectancy there has been an increase in the numbers of elderly people with difficult and demanding disabilities such as Alzheimer's disease that place great strain on those who care for them, so the cosy image of the happy extended family may not be a good description of many people's lives.

Many widowed elderly people prefer to live alone and be 'more independent'. This may be a result of earlier experience of the nuclear family and a wish to continue to live in their own homes. But they may also wish to have close contact with younger relatives, particularly grandchildren, so the stereotype 'round the corner' extended family of Young and Wilmott's *Family and Kinship in East London* in the 1950s may be an ideal to which many elderly people aspire today.

> *Is this a realistic possibility for many families? Think of the factors in industrial societies that can make this difficult.*

As they did in the past, grandparents and older relatives may be able to perform positive functions such as caring for the children of working mothers. Recent figures show that a large proportion of childcare undertaken for working mothers is carried

Most child care informal

Grandparents are the most likely carers for pre-school children, and fewer than one in 10 pupils under eight, are placed with a formal child carer, according to the survey which casts doubt on the Government's initiative to help poorer families with child care costs.

Under a scheme starting in October, people receiving family credit benefit, which tops up low pay, will be able to set against their weekly earnings up to £40 child care costs for under-11s. The scheme will be available only to families providing they use a registered childminder or day nursery.

Yesterday's survey of some 5,500 children under eight in 3,700 households shows that informal arranements remain the most common forms of child care.

Among pre-school children, 23 per cent were found to go to grandparents; 21 per cent were looked after by their father while their mother was out; 6 per cent were cared for by other relatives; and 7 per cent went to a friend or neighbour.

Only 8 per cent of pre-school children went to a day nursery and 6 per cent to a registered childminder.

Among schoolchildren under eight, 23 per cent were cared for out of school hours by their father, 15 per cent by their grandparents, 6 per cent by other relatives and 8 per cent by a friend or neighbour. Only 3 per cent went to a childminder and 6 per cent to a children's group.

The survey, by the Office of Population Censuses and Surveys, provides ammunition for groups pressing the Government to expand nursery school provision.

More than 40 per cent of mothers of children aged three or four not attending nursery school said they could have liked them to. Almost half the mothers of children attending playgroups would have preferred a different form of care, usually a nursery school.

Marion Kozak, co-ordinator of the Daycare Trust, a group campaigning for better child care provision, said: 'The survey shows how badly an overhaul of policy is needed.

'The stated aim of current policy is diversity and choice. But this research shows that parental choice is often an illusion.'

Guardian, 6 August 1994

out by grandmothers. Retirement as early as fifty in some professional occupations such as teaching could mean a new 'third age' role of daytime childcare while parents go out to work.

Young people in families

The demographic trend towards smaller average family size means that the majority of children have one or two siblings at the most, and the large family of six or more is now unusual. The communities that do have larger than average numbers of children tend to be those with strong cultural and religious traditions, such as Roman Catholics and Orthodox Jews.

Changes in the labour market and the extension of education to the late teens and early to mid-twenties have meant increased periods of dependency and residence in the family of origin. This can be a source of strain and tension between younger and older generations in the household (see page 145). Young people in such circumstances cannot generally support themselves independently, and within the home their role is still *ascribed* as it is with a child, despite their physical and sexual adulthood.

 Look up ascribed and achieved roles in your textbooks and briefly explain the difference.

Parents, and in particular mothers, may find it hard to cope with the stresses of work and the demands and consumption of a young adult at home.

Describe and make notes on the complications of interactions and roles between a mother and her adolescent son; compare them with the relationship between a father and his adolescent daughter.

Devise characters for a role play along these lines, and enact it in class or a small group.

Withdrawal of state benefits for 16–18 year olds, reduced employment opportunities and difficulties in obtaining housing extend the period of the younger person's dependency on his or her parents. Rising unemployment and reduced opportunities for graduates can mean that 'leaving home' to go to university may be only temporary as unemployment after graduation can result in a return to the parental home.

An alternative is the growth of more permanent rented accommodation for groups of young people living in student-type households and pooling their resources to keep costs low. More depressingly, the problems of living with parents may be a factor in the increase of homelessness among the young.

Ethnic minority families and households

The traditional sociological approach to the ethnic minority population in Britain was to focus on particular groups such as Afro-Caribbeans, South Asians and Cypriots and to use their supposedly 'different' family structures as part of the diversity argument to counter the dominant white stereotype of the nuclear family. However, there are many problems with this approach associated with over-generalization and issues of definition.

The following are two common stereotypes:

- Afro-Caribbean communities have a greater preponderance of single-parent families and absent fathers as a result of migratory patterns of male employment, resulting in strong matriarchal family units.

- The South Asian family is of the extended type, and individuals' wishes are secondary to family duties and responsibilities, in which the traditional arranged marriage plays a central part.

These statements are too sweeping, and they fail to recognize the shifting dynamics of family life and behavioural patterns in all communities in a changing society:

Afro-Caribbean families do have a greater proportion of single-parent families and absent fathers than the average for British society as a whole, but this difference is diminishing through time and could in any case be largely a result of poverty and job insecurity among males. Such factors also bear down upon all-white inner city areas such as the North East, as we noted in our earlier examination of the 'underclass' debate. In rebuttal of the irresponsible, feckless and unstable stereotype of the single-parent family, Sandra Wallman (1984) highlighted two Afro-Caribbean single-parent families headed by mothers which provided stable and secure homes supported by neighbours and the community (see page 92).

The majority of *South Asians* in Britain are Muslim, and their religion and culture provide clear guidelines as to family and kin responsibilities. Arranged marriages are expected for sons and daughters. However, a large proportion of young British Asians have been born, raised and educated in this country and, over time, expectations of marriage and family life have changed somewhat. One example is the shift towards negotiation between parents and offspring about an arranged marriage, so the prospective bride or groom has more say in the eventual choice of partner (see pages 119-22 for more on arranged marriages).

Housing types and size of accommodation in Britain, typified by the three-bedroom semi-detached, mean that newly married South Asian couples tend to gravitate towards nuclear family residence, often with financial support from the extended family. In more prosperous Asian families a house and car will be bought for the newly married couple. There is still close contact between extended family members and much mutual support is provided on the basis of duty to one's family. Family responsibilities are kept up over greater distances by weekend visits to towns such as Bradford, Leicester, Bolton and Blackburn.

The availability of higher education in universities has meant that young members of ethnic minority groups can travel and live away from their communities. At university they are likely to meet a wide variety of young people, with the inevitable possibility of marriage to someone of a different background. Difficulties can occur, as discussed previously (see pages 119-22), especially where there is family resistance, and inter-ethnic marriages are still unusual.

> *How 'different' from the dominant culture are ethnic minority groups in their marital and family patterns? Devise a table in two columns, showing points of increasing similarity in one column and differences in the other. Also make notes on possible differences between different ethnic minority groups.*

In the changing world of modern Britain it seems that the power of tradition is weakening somewhat in ethnic minority communities, and there is now greater variety of marital and family types than previously. In traditional white working-class areas such as South Yorkshire, Wales and the North East, the family structures and networks revolving around the extended family are very similar to patterns found in

Asian communities. In prosperous middle-class areas, more self-contained white and Asian nuclear families are to be found living next to each other.

Alternatives to the nuclear family

Relationships and number of partners

Alternatives to monogamous partnerships are to be found in many parts of the world in the form of *polygamy*, which is marriage to several partners. This can take the form of:

- *polygyny*, where a husband has a number of wives, as occurs in a number of Muslim countries and in African countries such as Kenya, or

- *polyandry,* where a wife has a number of husbands. This is much rarer, but it occurs among nomadic shepherd peoples in remote areas of Nepal and Tibet where several brothers will be married to one wife.

Less rigid versions of polygamy can occur in some tribes where group marriage is the practice. Before the imposition of British rule in 1792 the Nayars in India practised a polyandrous style of relationships in which young women took a number of partners and nomadic male soldiers had the right of choice of a number of eligible women in the villages they visited.

Childrearing patterns

The most widely discussed example of a non-familial system of childrearing is the Israeli kibbutz, which is a large commune usually centred around a farming or agricultural cooperative.

Figure 11.4 Non-familial childrearing in a kibbutz

The kibbutz system was established after the foundation in 1948 of the Israeli state, whose original guiding philosophy was socialism. The aim of the kibbutz system was to create equality between men and women by establishing communal childrearing so that mothers in particular were freed to work on the same basis as men. Children were brought up in separate children's accommodation, and although they would spend time with their parents every day there was no nuclear family unit as such.

Communes

In the 1960s and 1970s, communes were a feature of the 'counterculture' movement in the West, most often associated with hippies. They were established mainly by young people who saw themselves as 'dropping out' of mainstream society and its value system based on competition, consumerism and narrow self-interest. In the USA and Europe commune dwellers were often educated and middle class, former university students who had become disillusioned with the world of their parents. They were radical in their politics, responding to the Vietnam War with slogans such as 'Make love, not war'.

Self-sufficiency was generally a goal of commune-dwellers, so communes were often established on derelict farms and country houses with agricultural land. In Britain a number of communes were set up in the remoter areas of Wales, where such dwellings were readily available.

Part of the commune belief system involved extending the ideology of sharing material goods into the realm of sexual relations. Thus there were attempts to create alternatives to 'possessive' monogamy through promiscuous sex and group marriage, as well as communal living and childrearing.

Communes never became widespread as a form of social organization, but for a few people they pointed the way forward to a more cooperative lifestyle.

What do you think would be the advantages and disadvantages of living in a commune?

Current trends

In general, alternatives to the nuclear family have declined. Some alternatives, such as the Nayars' system of polyandry, have disappeared altogether. Polygamy is still an available option in many parts of the world, but in practice it is dying out as people choose monogamy.

Women are often a driving force behind such changes. For them polygyny and large household units often meant oppression and drudgery and in many cases jealousy between older and younger wives (in one African language the word for second wife is the same as jealousy). In the 1980s, the BBC TV series *Lovelaw*, which looked at marriage and family life around the world, found that women in particular favoured monogamy and considered the nuclear family as the ideal way to live. There remains a question whether this is an 'ideological illusion' fed by Western global media featuring romantic love as an ideal for true personal happiness.

Only around 4 per cent of the Israeli population now live in a kibbutz, and kibbutz dwellers are regarded as somewhat behind the times by the rest of the population, who desire to live more independently in towns and urban areas. In the kibbutzim that remain, it is now common for parents and children to have their own self-contained residential units, so to all intents and purposes they are nuclear families.

Communes based on hippie values of free love and self-sufficiency never became widespread, and unless they were based on strong values such as religious or political beliefs most were short-lived.

Why do you think this was so?

Today the 1960s version of communes tends to be an object of ridicule, since they are seen as naive. However, a continuation of this movement can be found among the New Age travellers or 'hippie convoys' which attracted generally adverse media and political attention in the 1980s and early 1990s. Travellers' groups played a central part in several campaigns against legislation such as the Criminal Justice Act of 1994 which limited many people's rights of access to land and freedom to travel. At the heart of the green movement (in campaigns against such issues as the building of motorways) and the animal rights movement (in campaigns such as the one against the export of live animals) that flourished in the 1980s and continue in the 1990s are young people who can be seen as the descendants of the 1960s commune movement.

The future of families and households

It is difficult to make clear predictions about future developments in families and households. However, it may be possible to use current trends and tendencies as a basis for suggesting some possibilities.

A useful starting point is the perspective of *post-modernism*, which has been the subject of social scientific debates in recent years. We cannot enter into detail about post-modernism here, but we can note a few outline points. Broadly, post-modernism rejects the notion that a future based on the recent past and current trends is predictable, a position that immediately sets it apart from traditional sociological approaches such as Marxism. Post-modernism talks of social developments in terms of *chaos* and *unpredictability,* and highlights *pluralism* and *diversity* as features of society.

Post-modernists disagree with the modernist view that societies are improving through time in terms of standards of living and lifestyles and that these improvements will continue into the future as more consumer goods and associated products are made available to increased numbers of the world's population. Here post-modernists concur with the *green* and environmentalist emphasis on the finiteness of the earth's resources. They believe that increasing numbers of people in both 'rich' and 'poor' worlds are entering an age of uncertainty.

In support of this position we can note that in industrialized countries there are rising levels of unemployment among all social groups, and a good education does not offer the same route to a secure professional career as it once did. Rising redundancy, unemployment, job-sharing, part-time work, short-term contracts and early retirement have reduced incomes and living standards for increased numbers of all social strata from the manual worker to the career professional.

Post-modernists also disagree with ideological and political 'meta-theories' and 'meta-narratives' that predict a better world in the future. Two of the most influential such meta-theories are Marxism, which predicts the eventual creation of a better life for all through socialism, and feminism, which looks forward to the ending of patriarchy and the establishment of an egalitarian society.

The concept of pluralism fits well into post-modernist thinking. In relation to families and households post-modernists tend to echo the 'diversity' argument, which expects that a wide variety of lifestyles and household types will come to characterize private life.

Future parenthood

Developments in genetics and associated advances in reproductive technology have been the subject of much attention in recent years because they seem to hold the potential for profound changes in parenthood and family relationships. In vitro fertilization and embryo transplants are among a number of techniques that have captured world headlines because of their implications for the future.

In 1994, a 62-year-old Italian woman gave birth to a son after treatment in a specialist fertility clinic (this was to 'replace' a 19-year-old son who had died several years earlier in a car crash). At the time of writing a 56-year-old British woman is undergoing the same treatment.

Discuss and make a list of the issues raised by such cases for family life in the future.

Single women and lesbians face test-tube baby ban

Lesbians and single heterosexual women could be prevented from receiving artificial insemination on the NHS in an attempt to reassert family values.

The Government is seeking ways to ensure that only married couples are helped to conceive a child at public expense, after several cases in which lesbian couples and single women received fertility treatment.

Tory MPs are concerned that public money is being spent in a way that could be seen as undermining the family. Ministers also want to place greater emphasis on supporting the traditional family after much embarrassment over the Government's discredited 'back to basics' campaign.

Mrs Virgina Bottomley, the Health Secretary, is considering strengthening Human Fertilisation and Embryology Authority guidelines to limit artificial insemination to heterosexual couples.

She may go further and restrict treatment to married people, although consideration is being given to unmarried couples in long-term relationships. A departmental source said: 'IVF is a scarce resource. It is not the business of the NHS to help lesbian couples to have children.'

Daily Telegraph, 8 July 1994

Eggs from an aborted foetus can now be used in fertility treatment and transplanted to the womb of a prospective 'host' mother. This development produced 'Your Mother Never Lived!' type newspaper headlines.

A number of lesbian couples in Britain have used artificial insemination, a technique that has been more widely available for lesbians in America. Applications for adoption have also been a way for homosexuals to become parents. The most common homosexual family probably involves a divorced or separated lesbian with children from a former heterosexual relationship.

Why do male homosexuals have greater difficulty adopting than females? Make a list of reasons.

The new reproductive technologies represent a challenge to the traditional concept of parenthood in relation to biological origins, sexuality and gender, and age:

- As in the case of the Italian woman, mothers may in future be as old as or older than grandmothers are today.

- Being raised by non-biological parents of the same sex may be one of several options.

- A child's biological mother may never have lived, in the case of egg transplants where an aborted foetus is the donor.

- Motherhood could occur 'post-career' in the fifties or sixties, so a life course could look like Figure 11.5.

Figure 11.5 Ageing motherhood? A future life course

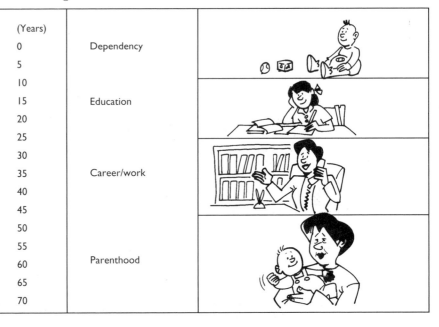

(Years)		
0	Dependency	
5		
10		
15	Education	
20		
25		
30		
35	Career/work	
40		
45		
50		
55		
60	Parenthood	
65		
70		

1 Is this a desirable development for the future?

2 Would it enable women to compete more equally with men in careers and occupations?

3 Examine why marriage, child-rearing and family life may presently be

barriers to women who wish to enjoy the same career and occupational
opportunities as men.

Marital stability

Increased rates of relationship and marital breakdown could indicate a future in which
serial monogamy becomes an established pattern. Some people might have a
succession of marriages, some might have several successive cohabiting relationships,
and others might experience a mix of both in the course of their lifetimes.

However, the rising incidence of AIDS and other sexually transmitted viruses such as
herpes may mean that, as well as safe sex practices, monogamy will become more
desirable for the protection of physical health and well-being, reinforcing the
traditional conservative and New Right belief that it is desirable from a spiritual and
moral viewpoint. In the British and American gay communities, which have been
severely affected by AIDS, the increased practice of safer sex has been accompanied
by a decline in promiscuity and the growth of stable monogamous relationships.

 *Do you think it more likely that monogamy or a variety of relationships will
become the commoner pattern in future?*

Some of the possibilities we have mentioned may seem to be far-fetched and more
in the realms of science fiction than fact, but they are arguably to be discerned in
trends and scientific breakthroughs that are already with us. In this sense the 'future'
of families and households is already at hand.

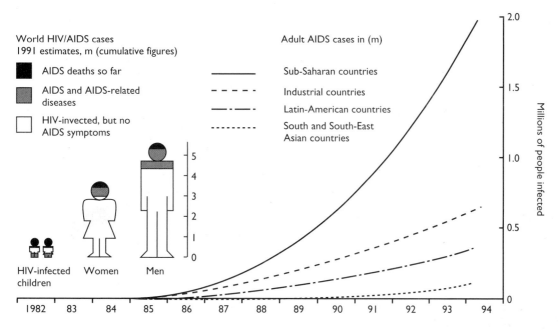

Source: *World Health Organization statistics; figure from The World in 1992 (London: The Economist Publications, 1991), p. 96.*

Figure 11.6 The spread of AIDS in the world: among men, women and children, and between groups of countries

Conclusion

In this book we have encountered a wide and diverse array of viewpoints, theories, approaches, perspectives, research findings and statistical trends on the subject of families and households. We live in a confusing and rapidly changing world with a range of possibilities, many of them worrying and potentially destabilizing for personal relationships.

Satisfying work for life, rising standards of living and health and a pollution-free environment may not be available for many people. In some ways this may strengthen the family and stabilize social relationships because in the confused and chaotic world predicted by post-modernist thinkers people may seek in their personal relationships the order and stability that they cannot find in their careers, work and living conditions.

In Britain, as Chester shows, a form of nuclear or neo-conventional family is the domestic arrangement that most people are likely to inhabit for the majority of their lives. But during their life course many people will also experience periods of change and instability such as divorce and a succession of partners.

Whether many people opt for monogamy and the nuclear family from choice or ideological pressure is the subject of continuing debate.

Whatever the future may hold for families and households, it is clear that most people in all societies seek love and acceptance from at least one other person; many gravitate towards the family for their sense of personal fulfilment and belonging, and as adults for a suitable environment in which to raise their children. It seems likely that the same needs will remain prominent for the foreseeable future; the sociological contribution is to recognize this while at the same time locating it within the context of variability, diversity and social change, as echoed in the trends examined in this book.

Private and personal lives in families and households involve highs and lows, tension and anxiety as well as exhilaration and happiness which are all part of this complex human structure called 'the family'. It has probably always been so, and will remain so for the foreseeable future.

Bibliography and further reading

Chester, R. (1985) 'The rise of the neo-conventional family', *New Society*, 9 May

Wallman, S. (1984) *Eight London Households*, London: Tavistock

Essay questions

1 'Ageing motherhood will be one of the most significant social changes to affect the nature of family life.' Discuss.

2 Examine some possibilities concerning the way people may live their personal lives and raise children in the future based on current sociological evidence.

Coursework suggestions

1 What do you see as the future for families and households?

2 What do you envisage will be your experience during your lifetime?

3 Consider any of the trends examined in this chapter – for instance, reproductive technologies – and conduct a detailed investigation to determine how such developments may affect family life in the future. You could conduct a social survey of attitudes to such issues.

Stimulus – response questions

Item A

The term Afro-Caribbean is itself problematic. It suggests birth in, and direct experience of, the Caribbean. Yet increasingly strict immigration controls have led to a decrease in the proportion of people of Afro-Caribbean descent who were actually born in the Caribbean. Over half of all Afro-Caribbean people are now not only British citizens but born in Britain.

The Afro-Caribbean family is discussed within British society as if it is uniformly working class. Yet despite their invisibility in popular and academic discourse, there are middle-class Afro-Caribbean families in Britain.

Black families of Afro-Caribbean origin live in various forms of household structure. By comparison with what is known about white households, little is known about black households. In 1982 the Policy Studies Institute surveyed a large representative sample of black people in Britain. Their report provides the best available picture of Afro-Caribbean families in Britain.

Two of the most widely believed characteristics of the Afro-Caribbean family for which there is some evidence are that first, it tends to be 'single parent'. Second that Afro-Caribbean mothers tend to be employed outside the home while their children are young. In many discussions of Afro-Caribbeans these features are reported to produce many of the ills of the black community.

It is however inaccurate to suggest that most Afro-Caribbean households are single parent ones, although the proportion of single Afro-Caribbean parents is high in comparison with white and Asian single parents. In the 1982 PSI survey, only 10 per cent of white households with children under 16 and 5 per cent of Asian households were headed by a lone parent, compared with 31 per cent of Afro-Caribbean households.

But does single parenthood have undesirable consequences for Afro-Caribbean children? Research by the Thomas Coram Research Unit showed no differences in achievement between children of similar social class whose parents were married and those with single parents.

Afro-Caribbean families violate dominant ideological assumptions about the correct situation in which to have children in another way. Black women of Afro-Caribbean origin are much more likely to be employed than their Asian or white counterparts. The PSI survey found that twice as many black women (41 per cent) of Afro-Caribbean origin were employed in 1982 as were white or Asian women. The majority of Afro-Caribbean women of child-bearing years were actually employed. If they were simply to leave the labour market and stay at home with their children they would substitute problems of poverty for problems of childcare. Both sets of problems are damaging to children.

Source: adapted from A. Phoenix, 'The Afro-Caribbean myth', *New Society*, 4 March 1988.

Item B

Popular images of the Asian family are often selective, prejudiced and riddled with contradictions. Even the term 'Asian' is misleading. It was a colonial invention. Few 'Asians' in Britain identify with the term. They prefer to see themselves as people of Indian, Pakistani or Bangladeshi origin or identify themselves as black people.

For anyone who cares to look, popular images do not match the reality. It is clear that Asian families show similarities and differences across as wide a range as others and that racism, class relations and the importance of gender and generation all have a bearing upon how families are formed.

The Asian population in Britain is over a million, with approximately 40 per cent born here.

There is great ethnic diversity among Asian people in Britain, including Punjabis and Tamils, Gujaratis, Goans and Bengalis.

Generally Asian households are larger with 4.6 members than white or West Indian households with 2.3 and 3.4 members respectively. Seventy-three per cent of Asian households include children (the figures are 31 per cent for whites and 57 per cent for West Indians). Overall the proportion of extended families is 21 per cent – higher than among other groups but not the norm. The trend is in fact towards nuclear families but this does not mean the importance of extended family ties has diminished.

Source: adapted from S. Westwood and P. Bhachu, 'Images and realities', *New Society*, 6 May 1988.

Item C

The term 'matrifocal family' will be used here to refer to female-headed families. In the USA in 1971, 29 per cent of all black families were headed by women. The high level of matrifocal families has been seen as the result of one or more factors. One argument accepts that poverty is the basic cause of matrifocal families but states also that matrifocality has become a part of the subculture of the poor. This view is contained in Oscar Lewis's concept of the culture of poverty. Ulf Hannerz argues that female-headed families are so common that to some degree they have become an expected and accepted alternative to the standard nuclear family. However, many sociologists view the female-headed family as a product of social disorganization and not, therefore, a viable alternative to the nuclear family. It has been accused of producing maladjusted children, juvenile delinquents and high school dropouts.

Source: adapted from M. Haralambos, *Sociology: Themes and Perspectives*, 2nd edn, London: Unwin Hyman, 1985

(a) Illustrating your answer with material from the Items above, explain why the authors of Items A and B consider the terms 'Afro-Caribbean' and 'Asian' inaccurate and problematic. **(5 marks)**

(b) Using material from the above Items and elsewhere, evaluate the extent to which popular images of ethnic minority households are 'selective, prejudiced and riddled with contradictions' (Item B, lines 2–3). **(8 marks)**

(c) Briefly explain the meaning of the term 'matrifocal family' (Item C). **(2 marks)**

(d) The author of Item C argues that 'many sociologists view the female-headed family as a product of social disorganization and not therefore a viable alternative to the nuclear family' (lines 14–18). To what extent is this view supported by sociological evidence? **(10 marks)**

General bibliography

Allan, G. (1985) *Family Life*, Cambridge: Blackwell

Anderson, M. (ed) (1980) *Sociology of the Family*, Harmondsworth: Penguin

Barrett, M. and McIntosh, M. (1982) *The Anti-social Family*, London: Verso

Berger, B. and Berger, P.L. (1983) *The War Over the Family*, London: Hutchinson

Boh, K. (et al) (1989) *Changing Patterns of European Family Life*, London: Routledge

Cheal, D. (1991) *Family and the State of Theory*, Hemel Hempstead: Harvester Wheatsheaf

Clark, D. (ed) (1991) *Marriage, Domestic Life and Social Change*, London: Routledge

Delphy, C. and Leonard, D. (1992) *Familiar Exploitation*, Cambridge: Polity Press

Drake, M. (ed) (1994) *Time, Family and Community*, Oxford: Blackwell

Elliot, F.R. (1986) *The Family: Change or Continuity?*, Atlantic Highlands: Humanities Press

Finch, J. and Mason, J. (1993) *Negotiating Family Responsibilities*, London: Routledge

Fletcher, R. (1988) *The Shaking of the Foundations – Family and Society*, London: Routledge

Gittins, D. (1985) *The Family in Question*, London: MacMillan

Henwood, M. (1987) *Inside the Family*, London: Family Policy Studies Centre

Morgan, D. (1985) *The Family, Politics and Social Theory*, London: Routledge

Rapoport, R.N., Fogarty, M.P. and Rapoport, R. (eds) (1982) *Families in Britain*, London: Routledge

Warde, A. and Abercrombie, N. (eds) (1994) *Family, Household and the Life-Course*, Lancaster: Framework Press

Wilson, A. (1985) *Family*, London: Tavistock

Young, M. and Wilmott, P. (1975) *The Symmetrical Family*, Harmondsworth: Penguin

Index